£400

W9-AAJ-814

Board
Overboard

Board Overboard

Laughs and Lessons for All but the Perfect Nonprofit

BRIAN O'CONNELL

Jossey–Bass Publishers
San Francisco

Substantial discounts on bulk quantities of Jossey-Bass books are available
to corporations, professional associations, and other organizations. For details
and discount information, contact the special sales department at Jossey-
Bass Inc., Publishers. (415) 433–1740; Fax (800) 605–2665.

For sales outside the United States, please contact your local Simon &
Schuster International Office.

▲
T**O**F Manufactured in the United States of America on Lyons Falls
Pathfinder Tradebook. This paper is acid-free and 100 percent totally
chlorine-free.

Library of Congress Cataloging-in-Publication Data
O'Connell, Brian, date.
    Board overboard : laughs and lessons for all but the perfect
nonprofit / Brian O'Connell.
        p.   cm.—(Jossey-Bass nonprofit sector series)
    ISBN 0-7879-0179-2 (alk. paper)
        1. Nonprofit organizations—Management—Anecdotes. 2. Directors
of corporations—Anecdotes. 3. Business meetings—Humor.
HD62.6.027   1996
658'.048—dc20   95-33964
                                                                      CIP

FIRST EDITION

HB Printing 10 9 8 7 6 5 4 3 2 1

Preface

Volunteering should produce results and inspiration. It should also be fun.

In previous books such as *Effective Leadership in Voluntary Organizations* and *America's Voluntary Spirit,* I've tried to share experiences and information that might contribute to increased performance and satisfaction. *The Board Member's Book* tried to do some of both and added a third part, called "Minutes of the Last Meeting," intended to provide a lighter moment. Out of those "minutes" grew this fuller glimpse of the hapless but humorous band of volunteers.

Much of the material presented here appeared in a subsequent book called *Our Organization,* published by Walker & Co. in 1987. I am grateful to that publisher for its willingness to revert all rights to me so that the laughs and lessons might continue to spread. I am also grateful to Alan Shrader and Lynn Luckow at Jossey-Bass for their interest and help in publishing this revised and expanded edition. Considerable thanks go also to Sharon

Stewart and Ann Brown O'Connell, who assisted and guided me at every stage.

In poking fun at my own kind, I draw on forty years of camaraderie and affection and an absolute conviction that ranking right up there with service and dedication should be that crazy extra thing called fun.

August 1995   Brian O'Connell
                                          Chatham, Massachusetts

TO THE VOLUNTEERS

*You are such a wonderful part
of the fabric and spirit of America*

*Any resemblance to any board
or board member I have ever worked with
is an unbelievable coincidence.*

ROSTER OF PARTICIPANTS

Officers

Mr. Rodney Russell
Chairperson

Mrs. Penelope Mitchell
Vice Chairperson

Mrs. Jeffrey (Effie) Black
Secretary

Hon. Peter Paul Henderson
Founder, First Chairperson, and Chairperson Emeritus

Mr. Harold Gonzalez
Treasurer

Board Members

Mrs. Carol Archer

Mrs. Louella Buckminster

Mr. George Colberg

Mr. Samuel Fales

Mrs. Patricia Greenlaw

Rev. Bryant Horsinger

Mr. George Horton

Mr. Bruce Knight

Mrs. Harriet Lortz

Mrs. Kathleen O'Reilly

Mrs. Gladys Pepper

Mr. Alan Scala

Mr. Joseph Shapiro

Ms. Beth Trister

Mr. Vincent Wenski

Mr. Paul Widen

Mrs. Felice Workenthrader

Mr. Cyrus Yarborough

Mr. Lucas Zukert

Staff

Mr. Jack Neal
Executive Secretary

Mrs. Paula Masonowitz
*Office Manager, Administrative Assistant,
Assistant Secretary, and Assistant Treasurer*

Order of Records from the Official Minutes of Our Organization

With an Indication of Some of the Setbacks,
Blow-Ups, Wild Schemes,
and Other Absurd Behavior
Encountered Along the Way

- *The matter of our Executive Secretary's salary is considered so confidential that the Board is not even allowed "twenty questions" to see if we can guess what the Executive Committee has decided.*

- *We debate and decide most matters relating to our forthcoming annual meeting, such as menus, parking, table decorations, and tipping, but leave details to the Planning Committee.*

- *A periodic visit from our national field representative reveals the good news that we are the only chapter in the country that has had its affiliation extended three times without meeting National standards.*

- *We are told that through National we can get director's liability insurance and are shocked to realize we have legal responsibility.*

- *There is a report of our exploratory visit to the Cutting-Edge and Fail-Safe Foundation, which concentrates on grassroots efforts to protect the ozone layer and gives priority to emerging organizations with a long track record.*

- *Our Executive Secretary reports on attendance at a Chamber of Commerce course called Sound Business Practices for Well-Meaning but Inept Nonprofit Managers.*

- *The year's delay in producing an annual report is because the advertising agency that agreed to do the layout on a volunteer basis got lucky and has some paid work.*

- *While in executive session, the Board also votes to move the office and revise the letterhead.*

- *In case the endowment doesn't build quickly enough to pay current bills, we also decide to launch a sure-fire bequest cultivation program called "Give as You Go."*
- *We tell our Executive Secretary that worrying us about unpaid bills interferes with the Board's positive karma.*

- *Once again our Treasurer sidesteps close review of current finances; this time he begins his report with the always more interesting topic of investment guidelines and time runs out before we can get to the red ink.*
- *Our approach to the Voluntary Action Center for a regular flow of clerical help is rebuffed because we are not committed to significant involvement and development of volunteers; we decide that we are not in tune with such radical notions.*
- *We debate the location of our new office and decide that we should strike a balance between appearing successful and being semi-seedy.*

- *The setting of Camp Bluebird takes us out of our everyday settings and routines, and we hate it.*
- *The local Volunteer Fire and Rescue Squad has its busiest weekend ever—and its most lucrative.*
- *Mrs. Mitchell is criticized for not putting her hidden dollars toward the rescue unit's final visit, but it is pointed out that with her personality, mad money is an essential commodity.*

1

Minutes of
Our January
Board Meeting

M r. Russell opened the meeting at 8:07 P.M. and immediately turned the meeting over to me, Mrs. Jeffrey (Effie) Black, Secretary of the Board of Directors, for the reading of the minutes of the last meeting. I announced that copies would be distributed at the conclusion of the reading. Mr. Scala asked if they could be distributed immediately so that we might dispense with the reading. I pointed out to Mr. Scala, as I had on several previous occasions, that *Robert's Rules of Order* requires a reading of the minutes. I also indicated that I had gotten out of a sickbed to fulfill this duty.

Mr. Russell suggested that we compromise by distributing the minutes in advance but still proceed with the reading, and everyone agreed. Mr. Scala, in a rare display of cooperation, complimented the Chairperson for having the diplomacy to propose what he called a "read-along." He suggested that for our next meeting we put the minutes to music and call it a "Minutes Minuet." Everyone chuckled. Mrs. Lortz said that any composition as long as my minutes couldn't be called a minuet. Nobody laughed. I read the minutes.

The Chairperson next called on the Treasurer to give the financial report. Mr. Gonzalez said that our income for the first six months of our July-to-June fiscal year was only $73,000, but projected receipts for the second half of the year were $809,000. Ms. Trister asked if this was realistic, but Mr. Gonzalez pointed out that as Treasurer, he dealt with expenses, not income. Ms. Trister apologized.

The Treasurer said he had heard indirectly that fundraising looked terrific. George Colberg asked if this was reflected yet in the financial statements. Mr. Gonzalez directed the question to our Executive Secretary, who said that bookkeeping was a little behind because our one-day-a-week bookkeeper/dictaphone transcriber/telephone operator/general handyperson had been on maternity leave and had just delivered a little boy. Everyone clapped and agreed to a resolution to send a letter of congratulations to the proud parents. A committee was appointed to select a gift.

The bookkeeping situation prompted Mr. Colberg to ask if we had an audit for the last fiscal year. Jack apologized, saying that we still don't, but added that we have to be patient because the service is being done for free by Mrs. Workenthrader's brother, who used to be an accountant but who is now in the Peace Corps and is away a lot.

Mr. Colberg asked whether Mr. Neal or Mr. Gonzalez had any general idea of what the income looked like in the half month since the December statement. Jack deferred to the Treasurer, who said that as manager of the branch where the association did its banking, he was aware that deposits were dropping off and that the Executive Secretary had inquired what a line of credit was. Other than that, he didn't know and would have to defer to the Fundraising Chairperson. Mr. Widen said he would prefer waiting to give his report until there was a more positive atmosphere.

Jack Neal said that he didn't want to ignore some rough patches in our financial picture but that he could confide to the Board that he had heard from an attorney in town that the association might be getting a nice bequest. In answer to questions, Jack said that he didn't know absolutely how much or how soon. This prompted Mrs. O'Reilly to ask if we knew whether the benefactor was dead yet. Jack said he had felt it was too delicate a question to ask. The Honorable Peter Paul Henderson,

Founder, First Chairperson, and Chairperson Emeritus, said he would check around to see if he could find out who it was and, if the person were still alive, whether we could hope that events might still help our cash flow this year. Everyone expressed appreciation.

Mr. Gonzalez said that on the expense side, things looked much better, that we were only 16 percent above last year's figure. Mr. Knight said that this was indeed good news, but didn't he recall that we had cut the budget by about 20 percent? The Treasurer acknowledged we had but explained that just because a Board cuts the budget doesn't mean that expenses go down. There was a long, thoughtful silence.

Mrs. Archer said she didn't know much about finances, but was she close to the mark in guessing that with income so far below expectations and expenses so far above budget, the picture was somewhat negative?

Mr. Colberg asked the Treasurer how he, from a banker's perspective, would assess the situation if income for the second half of the fiscal year was only as good as the first half and if expenditures remained at their current level. Mr. Gonzalez, responding in the professional spirit in which the question was asked, replied, "Stinky." In terms of figures, he indicated that the shortfall would be about $475,000.00 against reserves of $19,875.53. Mrs. Masonowitz, the Assistant Treasurer, asked what a line of credit was. To put things on a more positive track, Mr. Russell asked the Fundraising Chairperson to report.

Mr. Widen explained that there were some disappointments. To begin with, the Special Event, with a half-million-dollar goal, fell short. We had not been able to get Bob Hope, Frank Sinatra, Jack Benny (Mr. Widen complained that staff had not told him that Benny was dead), or their backup, President Clinton, and we had to settle for Merty Pink, the first woman deejay at station WOLP, who turned out to be less of a drawing card than was hoped. The event raised $783.87. Expenses were $1,113.53. But Mr. Widen said, "We got great publicity for the association, so the overall effort should be viewed as a long-term investment."

The direct-mail solicitation also came up short. Mr. Widen and his advisers had assumed that with the emotional pull our cause represents, plus the power of this Board and the success of so many less-worthy mail campaigns, we didn't need the ridiculous expense of a direct-mail firm or the loss of precious time in test marketing. Mr. Widen had volunteered to write the letters himself and to have them reproduced on his mimeograph. He reminded the Board that he had asked all of them to take a supply home and to mail them to all their friends. As of the meeting date, all of the returns were not in (thirteen of the twenty-four Board members had not yet mailed theirs), but, realistically, this part of the campaign would have to be viewed as a failure. The costs so far, not including staff time, were $1,756, and income was $98, not including an "in-kind" gift by the Fundraising Chairperson's own company. This gift was valued at $2,500 for reproduction, proofreading, messenger delivery, etc. Everyone thanked Mr. Widen for his personal generosity.

Actually, not everyone. Mrs. Buckminster asked Mr. Widen if the expenses included any reimbursements to his firm. Mr. Widen asked that the Chairperson rule the question out of order, rude, and hurtful. Fortunately, Jack Neal volunteered the information that Mr. Widen had given a great party for the guys and gals in his shop and in the association, all of whom had done most of the work on the mail appeal. Mr. Neal said that this extra effort on behalf of the campaign added spirit and thrust to the Fundraising Drive and therefore was not only in good taste but also entirely within accounting standards. Besides, he pointed out, many of the hors d'oeuvres were donated.

Mr. Zukert asked what the average contribution was from the letters the Board members themselves had sent out. The answer was $3.26. There was extended discussion about whether this was the result of the Board members' not having the right friends, not having enough friends, or, for the thirteen who had not mailed any letters, having no friends at all. After a heated exchange, it was agreed to refer the issue to the Nominating Committee.

Mr. Widen then reported on the part of the Drive involving contributions from the Board members themselves. He reminded the group that it was an axiom of Board membership that the Board exists to provide "wisdom, work, and wealth." The Honorable Peter Paul Henderson, Founder, First Chairperson, and Chairperson Emeritus, reacted, as he had on previous occasions, by saying that he found the phrase crass and undignified. Mr. Widen indicated that it was not necessary for Mr. Henderson to remind the Board of the value of his years of service involved in founding the association and guiding it to its current level.

The advance gifts solicitation from the Board was to have been the "leadership" part of the Drive but was not yet under way. It has been the major subject of seven Board meetings. Most recently, the Board has not been able to agree on whether there should be a suggested level or standard for contributions from the Board. This issue, in turn, has been subdivided into two issues:

1. Should the time given by Board members be considered in lieu of cash?

Mr. Russell, our Chairperson, is on record as saying that ordinarily the dollar value of volunteer time should not be considered but that in his case there should be an exception, particularly in light of how much time he is having to spend at the task. (It is assumed this would also apply to the demanding office of Secretary.)

2. Should "in-kind" gifts be considered?

Mrs. Archer has, on several occasions, reminded the group that while it was a pleasure to host the Board's Christmas party at her lovely home, it was still an expense that her husband's tax deduction hadn't begun to cover. Mr. Shapiro had told her that on that basis, he hoped the flowers the Board sent for the party had been treated as income. The resulting exchange was ruled off the record, but it led to a suggestion that the Board clarify its legal liability coverage.

Mr. Russell gave his regular speech about harmony and the joy of working together in a great crusade. (Please see any previous minutes for exact wording.)

After a cooling-off break, Mr. Widen continued his report on fundraising. He said there had been a few other setbacks. The telethon had turned out to compete with an unexpected seventh game of the World Series. To compound the problem, it had been carried on a cable channel not yet hooked up in our town (but several people in Charles County had said it came through loud and clear). The net loss was $9,828.41. Though the Fundraising Chairperson described the total as a disappointment, he felt that the experience and exposure would stand the association in good stead. He also said we may want to consider expanding to Charles County to take advantage of the softening up already accomplished there.

The door-to-door campaign had run into a discouraging obstacle. Mr. Widen and his campaign advisers gave long and careful consideration to the choice of a time when the most people would be at home, and they had been fortunate to get a permit for a Sunday. Mr. Widen indicated, with some pride, that obviously no one else had been alert enough to come up with the idea. The only disappointing aspect was that the committee had never in this world believed that 95 percent of their volunteers would be so disloyal as to stay home on Super Bowl Sunday. The net loss was $13,870.

Mr. Widen summarized that all in all, it hadn't been nearly as good a year as had been hoped. He said that perhaps in the remaining months they would be able to try some additional gimmicks. Mrs. Greenlaw said that she didn't think the association could afford any more fundraising.

Mrs. Lortz asked permission to bring up a timely matter and, with the Chairperson's assent, reintroduced her stale idea for an auxiliary. This time she emphasized the favorable fundraising role that other auxiliaries play for their organizations. With that comment, several Board members became rigidly alert. Mrs. Lortz said that there were certain ironclad rules necessary for the success of an auxiliary that, if followed, could result in thousands and, eventually, maybe millions of dollars for the association. She said that if this organization would provide the seed money to set up the auxiliary and would allow the auxiliary to be totally autonomous, she could guarantee results and might even be willing to head it herself. Mr. Gonzalez asked if the income of the auxiliary would go to the association, and the answer was decidedly affirmative, but only after the auxiliary's own projects were fully funded and endowed.

Mr. Colberg asked what the auxiliary would do. Mrs. Lortz responded that it would have its own bylaws, officers, board, bank accounts, and, as soon as possible, staff and office. "But what would it do?" Mr. Colberg persisted. Mrs. Lortz explained that until the auxiliary was established and its officers and board were in place, it would be inappropriate to speak for them.

The matter of an auxiliary was tabled.

Mr. Russell said it was time for committee reports.

The first report was from the Bylaws Committee, with Ms. Trister reporting for Mr. Fales, who was absent (due to personal circumstances different from the personal circumstances that kept him from the last meeting).

The Committee presented its seventeenth draft of the proposed Bylaws revisions, which have now stretched over four and a half years of study. At the Board's last meeting, some had objected to the language of proposed amendments to Article CXXVI, Section 78c (Removal of Committee Members) because it might have been construed to provide a Committee Chairperson with arbitrary authority to dismiss members who were consistently in the minority.

The new revised proposal included a new phrase: "Consistent losers, no matter how often on the wrong side, are protected by due process." To underscore this point, the Committee added a parenthetical phrase: "(This sacred institution, under God, shall be ruled by neither the tyranny of the majority nor the tyranny of the minority.)"

That amendment, as revised, was officially moved and seconded. During discussion, it was pointed out that the use of the term *minority* could be misread, and it was consequently moved to add the word *numerical* in front of both *minority* and *majority* wherever they appeared. The motion to amend the revised amendment to the Bylaws was seconded.

Ms. Trister reminded the Board that the Bylaws Committee had spent two evenings crafting this revised language and that she was not sure that she and Mr. Fales could hold the Committee together much longer if the

Board continued to behave like a board of editors rather than a board of directors, and on that basis, she flatly rejected any such amendment. Several members applauded.

Mr. Widen sympathized with the Bylaws Committee but said that in the spirit of democracy, bylaws should reflect the will of the governed. Several members clapped (including two who had already clapped on the other side). In this spirit, Mr. Widen offered an amendment to the amendment to the revised amendment to the Bylaws, which read, "Minorities reflected by numbers, race, ethnic origin, gender, sexual orientation, or Christian denomination . . ."

Mr. Zukert pointed out that not all religions are Christian and therefore moved that in the amendment to the amendment to the revised amendment to the Bylaws, "Christian denomination" be stricken. Mrs. Lortz moved that in the parenthetical section, the phrase beginning "This sacred institution, under God . . ." be dropped because it flew in the face of the separation of church and state. Mr. Widen agreed to accept her suggestion as part of his motion, but the seconder to Mr. Widen's motion did not, and therefore Mrs. Lortz asked that as a matter of principle, she, as a Christian herself, be the one to move that the whole parenthetical clause be stricken from the record.

A howl of protest erupted. Rev. Horsinger offered a Solomon-like solution in the form of a substitute motion that proposed that in the amendment to the amendment to amend the revised Bylaws, instead of striking the words *Christian denomination,* the word *religion* be substituted. Mrs. O'Reilly shouted that she sympathized wholly with Rev. Horsinger's intent but that it left a loophole wide enough for the devil himself to drive through. She asked if he would accept an amendment to his substitute motion so that instead of just "religion" the phrase would be "God-fearing religions, definitely not including some of the new weirdo cults." There was strong applause. Before Rev. Horsinger could reply, Mrs. Lortz was on her feet demanding that everybody was out of order until her motion of principle could be addressed.

To bring order to the chaos, the more experienced George Horton moved the previous question, but his intent was frustrated when Lucas Zukert asked which of the nine previous questions he was talking about. Pandemonium prevailed.

Finally, Mrs. Greenlaw, shouting above the others, demanded a point of personal privilege and, when recognized, said, "I move that I'm lost." Mr. Scala asked if he would accept an amendment to say "We are all lost" and said authoritatively that *Robert's Rules* gave this motion the highest order. Mrs. Lortz challenged whether a motion that "we are all lost" had a higher standing than a motion of principle, and Mr. Horton assured her that it did.

Ms. Trister said that because this item was only the first of sixteen recommendations of the Bylaws Committee to be considered by the Board that evening, she hoped that the Board would be willing for her to take all of these ideas back to the Committee and to come forward at another meeting with a proposal incorporating all of the various motions and ideas. Mr. Widen said if they could do that, they could leave God in wherever they wanted.

The Chairperson said that unraveling all these motions would have to start with the person who made the last motion being willing to be the first to back off so that the matter could be sent back to the Committee, and so forth down through each of the people who had made a motion. Mrs. O'Reilly said she would obstruct the process unless she was guaranteed that a Catholic would be added to the Bylaws Committee. In the interest of peace and sanity, Mr. Russell guaranteed that every person who had made a motion had a right to be certain that an individual of his or her political, philosophical, religious, or sexual orientation would be represented on the Bylaws Committee. On that basis, the unraveling proceeded.

Ms. Trister announced that the second item the Bylaws Committee was to bring before the Board related to whether the organization should use the term *Chairman, Chairwoman, Chairperson,* or *Chair.* Before she could offer her first motion, Mr. Russell gave the Board its choice of a recess, adjournment, or dissolution and fled the room.

On reconvening, the Chairperson said that in the interest of a change of pace, he was taking the privilege of moving ahead to the idea of having a "Board Retreat." Mr. Zukert kicked off the discussion about a one- or two-day retreat, when all the Board members would go off together to some secluded place to have a good block of uninterrupted time to really think about the state of the Association and to get to know one another better. Mr. Knight was concerned that his wife would be terribly upset about his participating in such a coed venture. Mrs. Greenlaw said his wife had no idea how safe she was.

Mr. Shapiro wanted to know what exactly would be accomplished during a retreat. Mr. Zukert pointed out that all of the Board's regular meetings were so taken up with the kind of important matters we had been discussing that evening that there was never a chance to really "brainstorm" or engage in "blue-skying." Mrs. Archer wanted to know how you got that kind of a process going, and Mr. Zukert indicated that most often it just starts with people talking off the tops of their heads. Mrs. Archer responded that this was not something this group needed to go away for two days to get good at.

Mr. Zukert asked the group to put aside immediate considerations and to try to see the idea from the point of view of the Board members' getting to know one another's strengths and weaknesses. Mr. Gonzalez said that that might be pressing our luck.

Ignoring these immediate doubts about the process, Mr. Zukert asked the group where such a session might be held. Four locations were suggested, but the reactions were so violently divided that Mr. Zukert concluded that a group that couldn't decide on the location for a retreat probably wasn't ready for one.

The final report for this meeting was by the Evaluation Committee and was presented by Mrs. Buckminster. She pointed out that the Committee deliberately included some "hard-nosed businessmen, as well as a number of social scientists and others who were used to getting to the heart of the matter." She assured the Board that the language of the Committee was laced with such concrete terms as *bottom line, cost effectiveness, management by objectives,* and *total quality management* and that this was one evaluation where just doing good was not good enough. For example, she said that one of the businessmen had been particularly helpful in pointing out that our program of public education would always defy quantitative analysis, and therefore we should drop any pursuits that can't be measured in specific body counts.

Rev. Horsinger interjected that it was wrong for a voluntary organization to sell its soul for the sake of doing something just because it can be measured. Mrs. Buckminster responded by asking the Reverend why he thought the Girl Scouts sell cookies.

Mr. Colberg said that if the churches had more doers and fewer worshipers or more sales than prayers, there would be a more businesslike approach to God, and a lot more souls could be saved per minister. The Reverend seemed moved by this admonition and asked how the idea might be implemented. Mr. Colberg said he couldn't be specific, but there was no doubt in his mind that churches and other nonprofit organizations, with all their bleeding-heart do-gooders, would be much better off if the people working in them had M.B.A. degrees rather than their abstract training in divinity, archaeology, social work, or library science. He capped his point by asking, "How many Bibles has theology ever sold?"

Mr. Russell asked what this hard-nosed Committee had concluded, and Mrs. Buckminster said that the findings of their two-year evaluation could be summarized as follows: "Any organization made up of such bright people, who are so dedicated and who have worked so hard, must be doing a great deal of good."

Some Board members wept.

On that positive note, the meeting was adjourned at 11:16 P.M.

Respectfully submitted,
Mrs. Jeffrey (Effie) Black,
Secretary of the Board of Directors

2
Minutes of Our February Board Meeting

M r. Russell began the meeting at 8:13 P.M. (though he had tried to start it at 8:04 and again at 8:10).

By prior agreement, negotiated among the officers since the last meeting, it had been arranged that minutes of meetings would be sent in advance but that the Secretary would present highlights before the floor was opened for comments and approval.

Only a quarter of an hour into my highlights, Mrs. Lortz interrupted with, "It would be less painful to go back to reading the blessed things!" I stuck to my side of the bargain. Indeed, I found that freed from the actual text, I could improvise with a bit of what my mother always said was my natural storytelling ability.

Mr. Gonzalez was not so fortunate. What started as a rehash of January's searing review of our finances took a surprising turn when Mrs. Archer switched the discussion to the terminology of the financial reports. She indicated, for example, that she had taken an "I'm OK, you're OK" course, which taught her that people shouldn't always start with negative thoughts. On that basis, she wondered why we couldn't make a point of beginning these discussions by looking at a piece of paper that just showed our income and assets without reference to any liabilities. Mr. Colberg responded that she was setting a trap for herself because what he was looking at in terms of income and assets was "not OK," and the liabilities were certainly "not OK," so one way or another we were going to get depressed.

Undeterred, Mrs. Archer said that maybe the problem would be eased if we stopped calling them liabilities. She pointed out that in the rehabilitation field, the professionals had learned long ago that any terms like *crippled* or *handicapped* or *disabled* just call attention to the negative, and they had learned to call such things *abilities* and *opportunities* and *strengths*. Warming to her topic and encouraged by the strong nods of Mr. Gonzalez and Jack Neal, who were pleased with any excuse to avoid the figures, she expanded on her ideas and said that all of our meetings get started on a negative note with our oppressive financial reports and that it would have a liberating effect, which might turn the association completely around, if we could find a way to emphasize the good news in our figures. It was clear that much of the Board agreed, but no one seemed to be able to come up with ways to do it.

Caught up in the spirit of this, Gladys Pepper suggested that we might use our problems to advantage if we would treat them as a spur to overcome our liabilities. Mr. Yarborough picked up the metaphor, but not the mood, when he held up the reports and responded, "If we want to look at it that way, I think our little junkie just hit bottom."

The discussion then zeroed in on whether it was best psychologically to present the reports early in the meeting, as a goad to progress, or to postpone them to the end of the meeting, where they wouldn't interfere with the good temper of the Board. After lengthy discussion, during which several members suggested that the reports be presented at about the middle of the meeting, it was agreed to appoint a committee to study the format, terminology, and psychological significance of our financial presentations. Mr. Colberg suggested that the proposed committee look also at content, but by then the Board had spent itself on the financial issues and was ready to move on.

At this point in the meeting, Mr. Wenski arrived and apologized for his tardiness. He explained that he had come home early to be sure to have ample time to get ready to be on time but started out watching the evening news at 5:30 and ended up watching two sets of local news, Dan Rather, and MacNeil-Lehrer, and by then he was so depressed he just couldn't get going. Mrs. Buckminster welcomed him to the 8 o'clock news.

Mr. Zukert said that whatever was decided about the financial reports, he hoped that they, along with the minutes and other materials, could be sent to the Board at least a week before the meetings. He said it was hard to deal with some of the issues without advance study. Jack Neal explained that this matter had come up often before, but, as he explained each time, his office doesn't get some necessary information until the last minute, and the crew doesn't really get geared up for a meeting until a day or even the evening before, so if they had to get everything out a week in advance, the meetings would have to be held a week later.

There was an unusually long pause, during which some people looked around for affirmation of the simple logic of this and others sought the opposite. Mr. Zukert started to sort it out but decided that somehow there had to be more to Jack's reasoning than appeared anywhere near the surface, and he thought it only fair to himself and to Jack to think about it before expressing a reaction.

The Chairperson, sensing that this was not the moment for objectivity, announced that he was taking the liberty of postponing the Board's scheduled session for evaluation of the Executive Secretary. (Mr. Zukert probably thought to himself that if he was right about the prior issue, they ought not to postpone the evaluation too long.)

On the general subject of materials for the Board, Ms. Trister, a new Board member, asked if the Board could also get minutes of Executive Committee meetings. A collective gasp filled the room. Paula Masonowitz, Office Manager, Administrative Assistant, Assistant Secretary, Assistant Treasurer, and oldest employee of the Association, went pale at the thought of what would happen next. Fortunately, and as further indication of why he is our leader, Mr. Russell was the first to recover, and while the others were too numb to react, he moved swiftly to gain control of the situation. He decided that this request could be dealt with only in the Association's tradition of minimum candor.

In measured tones, Mr. Russell explained that because the Executive Committee deals with so many sensitive matters, its meetings have to be off the record. He apologized but said that he was sure that as experienced volunteers, Ms. Trister and the rest of the Board would understand. He indicated that the Executive Committee had met eleven times since the last Board meeting and had worked very hard on behalf of the Board. Mrs. Archer asked if he could give some examples of what they had been doing, but Mr. Russell could only say that they had been dealing with across-the-board issues that had saved the Board countless time and upset. He would say that they covered such explosive and grisly topics as annual meeting speakers, approval of expense reports, reconciling of petty cash (including forgiveness of shortages!), approval of public positions and statements, disputes between the Chairperson and the Executive Secretary, and many other crucial questions. Mrs. O'Reilly asked, "What the hell are we for?" In the same patient way, Mr. Russell explained that "the Board is like a joint session of Congress, the Supreme Court, and the ultimate authority on all matters all rolled into one." The enormity of this example took the ardor out of what was the closest we would ever come to mutiny.

As feelings subsided, but before they were quieted, Mr. Widen asked, "If the Board doesn't know what's going on, how can it exercise ultimate authority?" The Honorable Peter Paul Henderson, Founder, First Chairperson, and Chairperson Emeritus, realizing that this was a moment for statesmanship, got to his feet and, once steadied, intoned, "The Executive Committee is there to handle all the really thoughtful and controversial matters that a large, unwieldy, and generally uninformed Board could never address with knowledge, experience, and time, but the bylaws and common practice call for there to be a Board, so that's why we have both."

Spent of wisdom and energy, our senior leader folded back into his chair. (In that instant it must have crossed Mr. Zukert's mind that maybe the evaluation should include Founder Henderson too.)

Mr. Scala asked if it was all right to know who is on the Executive Committee, and at least seven people shifted uneasily. Tiring of this continuing challenge, Mr. Russell responded somewhat testily that for the good of the individuals and the organization, and really for the good of every Board member, "The Executive Committee list is secret and will remain so." He returned to a more politic posture by adding that many of its members were present at the table at that very moment. An electric tingle vibrated through the room.

Mrs. Buckminster asked if, among the sensitive matters discussed and settled routinely by the Executive Committee, the Executive Secretary's salary had come up. Jack Neal slumped in a contortion of pain and fright. Mr. Russell said that he would not be revealing a confidence to say that this year they had done so, though usually the matter was referred to the even smaller Personnel Committee so that the smallest possible number would know. Mrs. Buckminster probed to learn what the salary was, and by now several others had joined Jack in body language that indicated horror and cramps. Sensing some small victory, several Board members pressed to gain at least an impression of the general salary range. To establish some sense of cooperation, Mr. Russell said that he could not answer the question directly, but he would give the Board three guesses.

"Under $100,000?" asked Archer.

"Yes," said Russell.

"Thank God," said Colberg.

"Does the figure we're talking about include benefits?" asked Zukert.

"Yes," said Russell, but added, "That's question two."

"Foul!" cried Zukert.

"Is it between $20,000 and $50,000?" asked Knight.

"Generally," said Russell.

And just before discussion was closed, Greenlaw queried, "Next time can we play twenty questions?"

The next matter involved selecting delegates for the state convention. Paula explained that ordinarily we would have five delegates, but because we are behind in our dues again, we only get two and a half delegates and two and a half alternates. George Horton wanted to know how in the world you could have a half delegate, but Felice Workenthrader replied, "All you need to do is attend one of those sessions and you'll know." Despite this characterization, competition for the available slots was intense. Before the sparring got unpleasant, we had to work our way through the formula of a half delegate, which produced a number of remarks that were intended to be humorous but bordered on the vulgar. Officials at the state office punished us more than they thought when they reduced us to a half delegate.

It was Harriet Lortz who finally suggested the solution of having the same person serve as both the half delegate and the half alternate. We were all so relieved that there was clapping and a cacophony of "Here, here." Alan Scala exclaimed, "With that kind of mind, maybe we've got ourselves a real Treasurer," and then, catching himself, he turned to a pained Mr. Gonzalez and said, "Just kidding, Harry." But the awkwardness around the table communicated a shared thought that maybe a new Treasurer was what we needed to make the figures better.

When the choosing got serious, it was obvious that, as always, Mr. Henderson had to be asked to lead the delegation. Only Chairperson Russell had the courage and quick-mindedness to suggest that our Founder could actually attend as an at-large delegate. Jack Neal coughed nervously, pointing out that while that was so, our budget did not cover expenses for at-large delegates.

This led Mr. Shapiro to ask what reimbursement we provided, and that led to a new discussion. We give seven cents a mile and thirty-five dollars per diem. After long and fruitless discussion, we acknowledged that although these fees are not altogether realistic, they are far more than we can afford. During the discussion, it was even suggested that we might ask the delegates to pick up their total expenses. Mr. Henderson's look of horror killed that idea.

Louella Buckminster said that the expenses would be eased somewhat if people doubled up in rooms, but Mrs. O'Reilly wanted to know what would happen if there isn't an even number of women. Rev. Horsinger raised his eyebrows, but Mr. Russell assured him that it was not that kind of convention. Under his breath, Alan Scala was heard to whisper, "The odd person gets Henderson."

Mr. Russell said that owing to a business conflict, he would not be able to go. Someone who wasn't thinking said that it would be logical for Penelope Mitchell to be next in line because she is our Vice Chairperson. It was left to me to point out that Mrs. Mitchell has missed four of the last six meetings, seven of the last ten, and twenty of the last thirty. Rev. Horsinger, in foolish fairness, said that this was a matter that the Nominating

Committee should resolve and that as long as she is our Vice Chairperson, she should have the chance. Because he had put it on such a high moral basis, no one wanted to take him on.

On the heels of this contention, the Board, with soothing unanimity, selected the Secretary for the other delegate's spot. My acceptance speech was warmly received.

It followed that Mr. Gonzalez, as Treasurer, should be selected as our half delegate/half alternate. Then, having covered the officers, the choices for alternates were particularly difficult. At one point, it came down to figuring the balance of men and women, and in an effort to give Mr. Gonzalez some choice in the matter, Ms. Trister asked Harry who he would want to sleep with. It was hard to know who was the more embarrassed.

Someone suggested that Harry Gonzalez and Jack Neal could sleep together, and that seemed to settle it until someone remembered that Paula is Jack Neal's staff alternate.

Vincent Wenski, who obviously wasn't at the last Board meeting and didn't read the minutes, said that he thought we should offer a chance to Paul Widen as a reward for his fundraising. It would be an extreme understatement to say that the suggestion was greeted coolly. For sixty seconds, no one moved an eye from the ceiling molding. Sensing that the wind was not likely to shift in his direction, Mr. Widen said that he just remembered he was going to have to attend a funeral that weekend anyway.

During the prolonged silence, it had become obvious that Founder Henderson was finding every conceivable way to make displeasure apparent, and it was then that we remembered we had not resolved the question of his role and expenses. At some risk, I suggested that he should take my place or Penelope Mitchell's, who had been absent so much anyway. The dilemma was solved when Mr. Shapiro suggested that the budget was already shot anyway, so we might as well pay Mr. Henderson's expenses as a delegate-at-large. Mr. Gonzalez came up with the unique idea of having Mrs. Henderson serve as one of our alternates, which would solve the problem of who Mr. Henderson would sleep with.

It was agreed that the final alternate's spot could not be decided until we knew who might not be going, what sex they were, who would still be available, who might be willing to pay their own way, and who would be available after all the above factors had been decided. With our earlier criteria in mind, Mr. Colberg said—and please note that I am quoting—"that any rich, bisexual half-ass would do." Almost everybody laughed. Mrs. Archer asked to be recorded as not laughing. Mrs.

O'Reilly, who had actually laughed, said that she should be recorded that way too. And as a courtesy, I've put Rev. Horsinger in that column, though I think I caught him smiling.

With the delegation pretty much decided, we moved on to the subject of our own annual meeting.

Mr. Fales, who had been excused from the last two meetings for two different but equally forgivable reasons, reported on initial preparations for the June "Big One," our fifteenth Annual Meeting. He said his committee was close to recommending people for awards but couldn't report on this until later. Mrs. Buckminster commented that after our marathon session on state convention delegates, we might not be ready for such discussions even by June.

The Board, as usual, did not involve itself with arrangements, but we were able to make some decisions on location, menu, price, parking arrangements, head table, ingredients for soft and hard punch, table decorations, name cards, table assignments, receiving line, guest list, photographer, location of registration table, and tipping. At our April and May meetings, when the event is closer, we will cover particulars. Details will be left to the committee and staff.

After a break, since it was getting late, we turned to two major items of business, the question of whether to explore membership in the United Way, and our Program Committee's report.

After our last fundraising report, several Board members had suggested that there must be an easier way, which is how the subject of the United Way got on our agenda.

Mr. Widen, Chairperson of this year's Fundraising Drive, inadvertently gave us our starting place for discussion when he said that to go in now would be to admit failure.

Right on the heels of that, Mr. Gonzalez contributed another unintended push when he warned us that going in could dry up all our other sources of funds. If a vote had been taken after those two arguments against joining, the vote would have been unanimous for signing on.

Mr. Yarborough said that we need to be prepared that the United Way would expect all Board members of a participating agency to contribute their fair share. Ms. Trister confirmed, from experience with another board, that the United Way's solicitation is so thorough that they actually study the giving records of agency trustees. On the basis of this important intelligence, the balance of sentiment careened to the other side.

For a while the spiral was downward. Of particular note was the experience that several Board members had had with the allocations process. They reported that in representing other causes, they had run into the horror of annual reporting requirements, hearings, reviews, and worse for every year's allotment. Mrs. Lortz gave some examples of the types of questions asked:

> How many people did you help? How much did you help them? What did it cost per limb or organ helped?
>
> If you are involved with mental health, how much better are they in terms of feeling good? Happiness? Fulfillment? Euphoria?
>
> Give approximate dollar cost per unit of feeling good, happiness, etc.
>
> List qualifications of your staff. List qualifications of your Board.

Mrs. Lortz said that these were just a few that she could remember but that she would get one of the seventy-two-page forms and send it over to Jack Neal. It was close to 11:00 P.M. when we finished the litany of horror stories about United Way participation. The low point in the discussion came when Mr. Knight reported that he had once been with an agency that went into the United Way and never came out!

Slowly the tide began to shift back. It actually started when Mr. Shapiro was arguing against joining because he said "they" would always be looking over our shoulder and telling us what to do.

Somehow that caused a few of the Board members to realize that if we had to tell them what we do, we might have to figure it out for ourselves, and maybe that wasn't all bad. Mr. Zukert mused that "maybe it would be a good way to get some training for Jack Neal or help in finding a new exec—if we ever needed it." Almost everybody nodded agreement until we realized that the only quiet head, bearing hurt, scared eyes, belonged to the object of our consideration.

By 11:30 P.M. the pendulum had swung back toward such favorable consideration that our attention had shifted to whether the United Way would take us in. There was general agreement that with our visibility and record it would be a cinch and that we should begin thinking primarily about our financial demands and other conditions.

We even seemed to get over the hurdle presented by Mr. Scala, who reminded us that the United Way had recently done a communitywide "needs assessment," which had resulted in the establishment of twenty-three categories, rated in order of priority. Although we didn't actually see ourselves in any of the categories, there was good reason to believe that we at least fell in between several of them.

After further discussion, it was agreed to "send out a search party," and we all raised our arms in a symbolic motion of "charge."

Unfortunately, the hour being as late as it was, the report of the Program Committee had to be postponed again.

Our Chairperson reminded everybody that at our next meeting we will have a guest from the National Office, who will tell us how we are doing compared to other chapters around the country.

The meeting was adjourned at 11:42 P.M.

Respectfully submitted,
Mrs. Jeffrey (Effie) Black,
Secretary of the Board of Directors

3
Minutes of Our March Board Meeting

Mr. Russell opened the meeting at 8:35 P.M., after we had punch and cookies to meet and welcome our National Office representative, Geneva Betts, who was seated on his left. He also pointed out that our Vice Chairperson, Penelope Mitchell, who sat at his right, was able to be with us after a few absences (four of seven, seven of eleven, and twenty of thirty-one!). I said that the minutes would record that the new members and even several of the old ones were pleased to know what she looked like. Mrs. Mitchell said it was a shame that such sarcasm was wasted on a readership of one.

I was about to disprove her point when, to my horror and humiliation, the Chairperson suggested that out of deference to Ms. Betts, and to be sure we provided enough time to profit from her message, we depart from our standard format and postpone the minutes and financial report until later in the meeting. I started to point out that at the very least not starting with the minutes was highly irregular and more likely in violation of state law and the Constitution, but Mr. Shapiro outshouted me with his demand to know if we were going to downplay and ignore those "blood-red numbers in the Treasurer's report." Mr. Russell ground his teeth into a smile and said that perhaps we might wait until our guest left to discuss personal matters.

Ms. Betts said it was all right because we should treat her as part of the family. Treasurer Gonzalez, sensing his reprieve threatened and speaking in the vernacular of family, told her to shut up and get up. Our Chairperson provided a more gracious introduction.

Geneva began by reminding us that she, too, had once been at the chapter level—in a state not far away—so she wanted us to think of her as the friendly big sister who, though she had gone on to National, still has empathy and sympathy for the local level. Penelope held a tissue to her eyes to keep from weeping, and Jack Neal held a handkerchief to his mouth to keep from gagging.

With one wary eye on Jack, Geneva said she liked to begin these reports with comments about all the positive things that the chapter is doing. There was a pained silence while she scanned her notes. Fixing on the one highlight she found recorded, she asked with the most upbeat tone she could muster, "I wonder how many of you realize that you are the only chapter in the country that has had its affiliation extended three times even though you've never met National standards!" We beamed at this honor.

Turning to other positives, Geneva told about the astounding growth rate of our nationwide crusade:

National income grew last year by 17 percent.

Membership grew by 22 percent.

Contributed radio and TV time was estimated by the broadcasting industry to be worth $506 billion.

Fifty-seven new local chapters were formed, bringing the new total to just under one thousand.

And six new states have been organized, bringing the total to fifty-nine.

With each announcement, the Honorable Peter Paul Henderson, our Founder, First Chairperson, and Chairperson Emeritus, slumped deeper into his chair until his eyes were barely level with the table.

Then there was a litany of success stories about other chapters, filled with doubling or quintupling income, membership growth, surges of publicity, program impact, and on and on. One of our new Board members made the mistake of asking how we compared. Geneva reacted like a supervisor in an employee evaluation who has just begun trying to soften the blow before putting the person on probation, when the employee asks, "What about my raise?" With aplomb Geneva recovered, and taking advantage of the opening, albeit premature, said, "It's curious you should bring that up." She began with comparisons, moved to contrasts, and then slid into the vernacular of day and night. In fairness, she did it with candor, grace, and even humor, though some of her "good news/bad news" stories left us little doubt which side we were on.

At one point, for purposes of encouragement, she compared us with the Adams County unit—her one big mistake of the evening. She evidently pierced deep into the competitive instincts of our otherwise implacable leader, who for a moment lost his aplomb and, jumping to his feet, shook his finger at poor Ms. Betts and wailed, "Sure, and it's headed by old Mrs. Richbitch Gotrocks who pours in money and gets all of her friends to do the same, and then they have charity balls and get their pictures all over the paper, and . . ." Catching himself, he apologized and sat down. Geneva got the point.

Ms. Betts was a bit more judicious in the selection of her second comparison, but when she described the particular chapter, it was obvious that the secret of its success was that it had a highly qualified board, which caused George Colberg to comment, "Oh, that explains it." In frustration, Bruce Knight said that these examples weren't fair because they involved exceptional people, and Geneva should understand that, with no apologies, we accept ourselves as average. Warming to the point and wishing to put ourselves in better light for fairer comparison, Mr. Widen said, "We're even below average." There was a silence ripe with ambivalence. It is to Ms. Betts's distinct credit that she didn't take advantage of the opening.

Her third selection was more appropriate. At least it was farther away. She outlined the work of the Washington County chapter in Maryland and said that we might model ourselves after it. She said she'd even taken the liberty of suggesting to the Maryland group that it enter into a "mentor" relationship with our chapter, and the group was willing. To her disappointment, this didn't go over too well on our side. Mr. Yarborough said that the last time he had a tutor, he flunked the subject, and besides, her breath smelled. Mrs. Archer, who is heading our exploratory committee with the United Way, said we were already having enough trouble trying to explain ourselves to outsiders, who seem to begin the relationship with an assumption that we are idiots. Mr. Horton said that he bet the Washington chapter got so good by going around stealing other people's secrets. In the only time that evening that she blew her cool, Ms. Betts retorted, "Coming here would be rather barren foraging."

While on the attack, she took up the matter of the sloppiness, casualness, and even flippancy of our required reports to National. For example, she held up the thirty-nine-page program report form for last year, on which the only thing written was, "If and when our Board ever gets off its duff and does something, we'll have something to report." All eyes glared at Jack, who twisted grotesquely as he retched his way to the men's room.

It was finally obvious that our Executive Secretary was not going to return right away, so the meeting proceeded without him. Ms. Betts reported on the recent National annual meeting. There had been several controversial resolutions, which occupied hundreds of hours of debate. The major one, still totally unresolved, had proposed that all the units of the organization adopt a common name. This had come up two years ago, and a study had been called that showed that out of more than 500 chapters responding to the survey, there were 428 different names. There were groups, colonies, assemblies, congregations, bands, troupes, troops, centers, federations, caucuses, conferences, clans, in groups, out groups, conventicles, festivals, movements, fraternities, meeting grounds, and one that just refers to itself as "Our Organization."

There were two parts to the proposed resolution. The first called for agreement that there should be a common name, and this passed within minutes. The second proposed one of three suggested names, and after 490 proposed substitutions, the study committee was extended for another two years.

Another resolution had also sought commonality and unity. It called for having one clear-cut national program priority for the whole organization. It was pointed out that if we did this, the whole organization would be moving in lockstep, which was the secret of all great national crusades. Here, too, everyone agreed with the purpose and everyone disagreed on what the number one priority should be. In this case, though, a compromise resolution was accepted: "We, the Delegate Assembly, speaking with one unified national voice, hereby vote that each chapter, consistent with local circumstances, finances, customs, and idiosyncrasies, must give at least some thought to paying some attention to one or more of the forty-three program emphases adopted as first priority by this body."

Geneva said that the only resolution that took even more time than those two involved trying to agree on a change of fiscal year. With our year-end financial figures in mind, Mr. Colberg asked if the resolution included the possibility of having more than twelve months in a fiscal year. Unfortunately, it does not, but our National representative said that the resolution had been tabled and that when it came up again, she would propose this as a forty-seventh amendment.

There was one resolution that some of us thought pretty silly. There evidently was a proposal to have five National Vice Presidents rather than three, with each identified as first, second, third, and so forth. Mr. Fales said this was a waste of time, and in any case, who in the world would want to be known as the "Fifth Vice President"? Mrs. Mitchell leaned over and, smiling at Geneva, said, "Each of us should be prepared to do whatever is necessary to help the organization."

One resolution got a predictable response. It proposed that the Delegate Assembly and the National Board, now approximately 85 percent male, should be required to have closer to a fifty-fifty balance. It was defeated by approximately 85 percent of the votes. Ms. Betts said it would be brought up again next year.

On that note, the group gave Geneva a round of applause, and with that we broke to finish the punch and cookies.

When we resumed, Mr. Russell noted that Mr. Wenski had joined us. He apologized for being tardy, saying that he had to be with a woman whose husband had been kidnapped, leaving her distraught. Mrs. O'Reilly observed that it obviously wasn't his own wife, and the meeting returned to its normal tension.

I suggested that this would be a good time for the minutes, but the Chairperson rushed on. Mr. Scala, thinking he was being funny, said that maybe I could mouth them while we were hearing other reports, and Penelope Mitchell chimed in, "That would indeed be a minimal subliminal." I decided to bide my time.

There was a report on awards from Mr. Fales of the Annual Meeting Committee.

He passed around a list of the honorees, including twenty-six groups and thirty-three individuals. Most of the discussion that followed could be compressed to "Why, why, why?" or, more fully, "Why this one? Why that one?" Mrs. O'Reilly summarized the sentiment of the Board: "There is hardly a damn one of them who has lifted a finger." Mr. Fales reminded the group with patience and pedantry that "awards are either for getting people out of an organization or for sucking them in." That stopped most of us.

Rev. Horsinger, with his usual naïveté, asked why all the newspapers and radio and TV stations were getting awards again this year when they hadn't yet given us any coverage. Picking up Mr. Fales's tone, Pat Greenlaw, speaking for the Public Relations Committee, said, "If we don't honor them, they never will."

Ms. Trister noted that we were giving awards to all the volunteers who had given more than fifty hours and, with demure innocence, asked if that included Board members. Mr. Fales explained that the awards were reserved for volunteers. Beth looked quizzical but didn't press the point. (She told me later that in a future meeting she wanted to bring up the distinction between volunteers and Board members and even between Board members and staff, but I told her she was heading into very deep water.) Mrs. Lortz thought it was great that we were honoring these volunteers but felt it was a bad signal to be spending money on them. She thought that might interfere with the image of them as volunteers. Others said that it's the only thing we can give them to show our appreciation for all the free time they donate. It was agreed to go ahead with the awards but to not spend more than two dollars apiece. Mr. Horton snorted that with all the volunteers he had seen around, this might add up to four dollars.

Reflecting the good vibes at the close of Geneva Betts's report, and for other reasons not appropriate for minutes but probably obvious anyway, Mrs. Mitchell suggested that it would be a novel idea for us to give an award to the National Office. After all, she said, "They're always giving awards to chapters for best this and that, so why don't we turn it around and give them something?"

Mr. Gonzalez said that from the mail he's been seeing, they would rather have money. Mrs. Pepper asked what we would honor them for, and there was a silence while we brainstormed. You could almost hear the buzz of minds at work.

After several minutes with not a single idea produced, Mr. Zukert offered, "We could give it to them for courage in keeping us affiliated." A committee was appointed to continue the brainstorming.

As always seems to happen, the Board spent what seemed like half the meeting talking about publicity for the Annual Meeting, and as usual there was a tug-of-war between Pat Greenlaw of the Public Relations Committee and Sam Fales of the Annual Meeting Committee as to who should lead this part of the discussion. The two did agree that if someone like the Governor comes, much of the publicity will be handled by his staff, and our Chairperson tried, quite unsuccessfully, to leave the matter at that.

Mr. Wenski said that with all the media there to get their awards, publicity would pretty much take care of itself, but all of us recall the low point of last year's meeting when name after name was called, and the only award acceptance was by a woman whose son had once been a copy boy down at the *News.* Some of the weeklies do cover the story but never mention much about the meeting or even the other award winners. They generally make it sound as though they had been singled out for a Pulitzer, but it's to their advantage not to make too much of the sponsor.

Pat Greenlaw complained that she couldn't be expected to get publicity if the association didn't generate interesting activities. Sam Fales countered that it was his understanding that good flacks have a nose for publicity and can generate it out of everyday happenings. Greenlaw countered, "It would make my day if one of your annual meetings could at least be ordinary—they're so damn dull that if Dan Rather attended, he'd have to call off the next day's evening news."

For the tenth year in a row, our long Board discussion of Annual Meeting publicity had aimed high—and crashed.

Mr. Russell asked Mrs. Greenlaw if she was ready to give the rest of the PR Committee report, and she said she wouldn't dare.

We then took up the twenty-first report of our Task Force on Improving Performance. Its leader, Mr. Horton, reminded us that we had already invested considerably of board and staff time and even some of our actual resources in a number of activities, including these:

- A six-month crash course on Management by Objectives (it crashed)

- Intensive submersion in Zero-Base Budgeting (zero results)
- A year's preparation for Total Quality Management (we couldn't even master the initials *TQM*)

Mr. Horton indicated that it was now clear to Task Force members that we should have started with something even more basic, but they couldn't find a course that came down to the Board's low common denominator.

Into that vacuum swooshed several board members in a cacophony of shouted proposals including yoga, Zen, tai chi, and meditation and descending to astrology, yin-yang, tarot, and palm reading.

Each has its vocal proponents, but none commanded anything like a majority until Penelope Mitchell, of all people, said, "What about prayer?" At first there were only good-humored smiles, even from Rev. Horsinger, but then Mrs. Workenthrader asked if Mrs. Mitchell was possibly serious. With that opening, she elaborated, "Throughout history," she began (and I steeled myself for one of her endless monologues, which I shall try valiantly to summarize), "when tribes have faced hopelessness and despair, they have joined hands and minds and spirits in urgent, desperate, pleading prayer, and when they raised their heads and opened their eyes, there was light, and the way was clear."

"My God," wept Mrs. O'Reilly.

"Precisely," responded Rev. Horsinger.

And by acclamation, we agreed to put the issue of our improvement in God's hands, aided by a commitment to begin future board meetings with prayer.

Mr. Colberg was skeptical but ambivalent. "Nothing else has worked, so what the hell," he figured.

Mrs. Greenlaw hoped he hadn't broken the spell.

On the chance that God was not on our side or needed some sign of self-help, Mr. Knight said we should plan to take advantage of an opportunity being provided by the Chamber of Commerce for orienting and training agency staff about good corporate practices. The course is called Sound Business Practices for Well-Meaning but Inept Nonprofit Managers.

Mr. Knight made our decision easy when he said that the course was being paid for by the various large firms that would be demonstrating their wares and services. We voted for it in a flash.

This part of our meeting ended with good feelings about our stewardship. With God and big business behind us, we couldn't help but improve our performance.

Mr. Widen then reported for the team that had been chosen to make an exploratory visit to some of the foundations in town. The team's initial visit had been to the Cutting-Edge and Fail-Safe Foundation (CEFS). Team members learned that for the exploratory session, at least with the CEFS, you don't actually see a person. At this stage it's entirely automated. As Mr. Widen explained it, "In the lobby there is a machine that is activated when you open the door. It provides a history of the foundation, including the founder's early years, courtship days, background on how he made so very much money—mostly brilliance, persistence, clean living, and a partnership with his wife (who didn't seem to be the same woman he had courted), and the donor's philosophy of philanthropy: 'We give only to those who are very needy, aggressive, bright self-starters who can pull themselves up by their bootstraps.' The words and the voice discourage anyone who doesn't qualify from going the next step. Our team found itself wondering how many people fit those criteria and are still very poor, and we guessed that's why the foundation has so much money.

"We decided that as long as we were there, we might as well proceed, so we punched the obviously hardly ever used button number two. This produced a printout of the foundation's fields of interest, which was followed by a running listing of the things the CEFS doesn't fund. There was so much to absorb in both these sections that when it was over, we punched number two again and tried to take notes of as much of the fifteen-minute presentation as possible.

"As nearly as my records can tell, the foundation is interested only in local projects, the closer to the neighborhood the better, that have the best chance of protecting the ozone layer.

"That was pretty straightforward, but the don'ts were harder to keep track of. The foundation has one of those annual medical-exam forms that ask you if you have had all the diseases of the world and has added an indication that of all these, the foundation supports only terminal illnesses, which we thought an odd way to express it. So much for the first section.

"The second indicated that the CEFS does not support institutions, organizations, associations, or individuals, nor does it provide collaborative support to projects of other funders.

"Thinking that we might slip in by calling ourselves a team, we took note of the other exceptions, which fairly narrowly identified such factors as age, gender, geography, education, sexual orientation, hobbies, physical attributes, IQ, and several other things.

"By the time we got to button three, we were a bit discouraged, but we were glad we hadn't given up. The button was stiff from disuse, but we jiggled it free and heard a recorded message congratulating us on our extraordinary uniqueness. It ended, 'We think the founder would have liked you.' With that, we were given a choice of filling out a multiple-choice questionnaire or writing an instant essay. We all agreed that there being three of us, we'd have a better chance at multiple choice, so we pushed button four."

At this point, Mr. Widen showed us a few of the pages that popped out:

1. We are an organization qualifying as:

   501(c)(3)

   501(c)(4)

   501(c)(7)

   All or none of the above

   We have our IRS letter to prove it.

2. We have been in business:

   500 years

   100–500 years

   50–100 years

   We are an emerging organization.

3. Our role is:

   Direct service

   Advocacy

   Activism (If you check this box, don't bother to fill in the rest. We know your type.)

4. This project is for:

   Demonstration

   Demonstration and feasibility

Demonstration, feasibility, modeling, and pilot

None of the above, but we're innovative

5. Please stipulate that on the basis of preresearch, it is predictable that the project will do exactly what it says it will do—for example, the project is actually finished, but it turned out so well that you think someone should have supported it in the first place. Please do not be afraid to be truthful. We like to back winners.

6. How would you describe the project?

A gamble

A flyer

Far out

Please do not hesitate to check one of the above. This is the first item we look at, and it can save us all a lot of time.

"At that point we decided to do the essay," said Mr. Widen. For ease in reporting, Mr. Widen and his team provided their essay, which follows:

Our Organization is somewhere between emerging and well established, but our grass roots already run deep and wide. We are innovative but hold to traditional values. We are daring but do not gamble. We do not believe in jargon or obfuscation. We are straightforward, solid, middle-of-the-road edge-cutters with a record of feasibility pilots that model the best of demonstrations.

We do not seek project support that masks an underlying intent to build endowments or reserves, and we don't kid you with such blanket categories as contingency funds and demonstration projects. In perfect candor, what we seek is a plain ordinary slush fund.

We know that slush funds have gotten a bad name, but if you look at all the great organizations—Harvard, the Metropolitan Museum of Art, Colonial Williamsburg, the Council on Foreign Relations, and all the rest—what they all have in common are liquid slush funds.

Any foundation worth its salt has its own slush fund—sometimes called the Officers' or President's Discretionary Fund.

Though the beauty of slush funds is that they trickle away, we are grant-smart enough to know that we should try to tell you what we would do with it, which, of course, we don't know, which, of course, you know—all of which we both know.

A flexible, dynamic organization shouldn't try to foresee what's ahead but must be ready to respond to the challenges and opportunities of the moment. Who would have planned or have been ready for the eruption of Mount St. Helens?

We can assure you that whatever unanticipated purposes we put your money toward will involve projects that can be replicated for meaningful implementation, employing the expertise of everyone in the community.

Right now, all of our ideas seem to need nourishment, and, in keeping with the example and symbolism of the Green Revolution, good ideas, like crops, need the waters of spring, which, of course, come from mountain slush. Look upon our application as the Future Springs of Mount Everest Slush Fund.

You can be assured that the Board and staff of Our Organization are made up of average, middle-of-the-road plodders who are the type that de Tocqueville said made America what it is and that have produced our country's pathfinders and explorers. Please do not turn us down because we are not already a rich, successful organization. Keep in mind that before he took his flight, whoever heard of Lindbergh? And he didn't do it in some fancy multiengine jet. He chose a modest single-engine prop plane. That's our stage and style. You might even think of us as the Future Springs of Mount Everest Slush Fund to Nurture Budding Lindberghs.

Lastly, we can assure you that no part of the grant will be used for overhead or fundraising costs. It will all be pure program expense composed of nothing but salaries and travel expenses and other basic costs of innovation.

If you need elaboration, let us know, and we can shift some of the sentences around.

If you need a specific budget, we can make that up.

Please send as much as you can as soon as you can.

We are a public charity with 501(c)(3) status in reasonably good standing with the IRS.

Mr. Russell thanked Mr. Widen and his courageous team for their efforts to date. Mr. Gonzalez asked, "What happens next?" Mr. Widen indicated, "If we pass the first stage, we get to meet a real person at the foundation." Louella Buckminster was so impressed that she wanted to know if we could all go. Mr. Widen downplayed the appointment and said that our team would probably just meet with a program officer. Mrs. Buckminster reacted, "That's still a lot better than an enlisted person or a civilian."

Mr. Colberg wanted to know, "How much are we asking for?" Mr. Widen explained, "We don't want to put in a specific figure because you usually get only half of what you ask for, and we're hoping for twice as much."

With the hour approaching midnight, Mr. Russell suggested that we reluctantly skip the Program Committee report, the minutes, the Treasurer's report, evaluation of the Executive Director, and selection of the new Fundraising Chairperson. Recalling Jack Neal's note on our program report to National, Mr. Colberg commented, "The SOB was never so lucky." Mr. Widen was concerned that the organization would try to go as long as two months more without a new Fundraising Chairperson, but Bruce Knight assured him that with all the money we would be getting from the United Way and foundations, we might not need a Fundraising Drive.

Despite the hour, several members were stunned that we would not get to the Treasurer's report. We would have been there until morning, but Mr. Russell reminded everyone that Mr. Gonzalez is bonded and that through National, we have directors' liability insurance for the Board.

We were shocked to realize that we have any legal liability for what goes on. We demanded that this topic be put high on the agenda of a future meeting.

I tried with all my might to get them to hear the minutes of the previous meeting, but all I could get was the Chairperson's assurance that very early in the next meeting we could have the minutes of the two previous meetings. I said it would be unconstitutional to do it that way. I thought Mr. Scala was about to agree with me

when he said that he, too, thought it would be unconstitutional. "But," he added, "it will place us all in double
jeopardy."

This unofficial meeting was adjourned at 12:01 A.M.

> *Angrily submitted,*
> *Mrs. Jeffrey (Effie) Black,*
> *Secretary of the Board of Directors*

4

Minutes of
Our April
Board Meeting

W hen asked to read the minutes of our last two meetings, I explained, just as I had in writing immediately following our informal gathering in March, that our failure to read and act on the minutes of our February meeting disqualified both sessions as official. Mr. Russell cajoled, and Jack Neal pleaded, but I would not be budged. As far as I am concerned and as far as the records go, there was no February meeting and there was no March meeting; therefore there are no minutes to read.

I'm sure there was far more panic about the non-meetings than showed, but given the packed agenda, we moved on.

By tacit approval of all present, we agreed that the minutes of this meeting should not record our prayerful beginning, which was marred by jockeying for who would hold—or not hold—whose hands and by Mrs. O'Reilly's suggestion that God is most likely to listen to those who have been to confession and so we should start there.

Thinking that she meant that we should let it all hang out, it was clear that there were many immediate and urgent prayers offered up but few related to Our Organization, except perhaps that Mrs. O'Reilly drop dead. In any case, God provided relief by arranging that Mrs. O'Reilly's suggestion should fail for lack of a second.

We agreed that we need to rethink the idea of prayer sessions, and Rev. Horsinger volunteered to prepare other ideas for getting divine intervention.

Chairperson Russell called on Jack Neal to report what he had learned at the Chamber of Commerce course, Sound Business Practices for Well-Meaning but Inept Nonprofit Managers, and asked him to focus on things that would help improve our performance.

To provide assurances that the course was no boondoggle, Jack said that it was very hard work, that he had learned a lot, and that as indicated previously, the course was absolutely free thanks to the generos-

ity of some of the big national firms that do business
in our community.

Jack was also careful and clever in his initial examples. He deliberately mentioned proposals he had heard
that would have special appeal to board members—for
example:

- Computer modems, printers, and E-mail capacity
  for everybody, including board members
- A computerized accounting system, with oversight
  supervision by a partner-level CPA (even Lucas
  Zukert looked pleased).
- Video telephones and capacity for teleconferenc-
  ing, which could mean that many of our meetings
  might be held without coming to the office.
- Full travel services for both board and staff, including discounts on vacation planning, and member-
  ships in twenty-nine airline clubs and fifty-two
  frequent-flyer programs, with bonus miles for the
  person doing the bookings (Paula Masonowitz
  beamed, but I'm sure there will be agreement that
  this burden should fall to the Secretary).

Jack paused, but not so long as to let financial considerations come to mind or at least to the surface.
Encouraged, he pressed on with other recommendations

made by the firms that had made this wonderful course possible.

- Complete orientation to the multiple advantages and savings inherent in having mainframe computer capacity, provided by a firm that deserves to be named but in the interest of fairness to all our supporters—or at least potential supporters—should not be singled out (but one that we could probably guess anyway). For smaller organizations, payments can be spread over seventy-five years.
- Personnel record keeping that would cover payroll, benefits, sick leave, earned vacation, and much more. The recommended system includes all necessary training, equipment, software, and maintenance.

By this time, Mr. Colberg had begun to have doubts and asked why we would need this additional equipment for personnel functions if we were already going to have a mainframe. Jack responded with confidence and logic that at this stage, the two systems are not compatible, "so we'll need both." With Mr. Colberg's hand up and mouth open, Jack rushed ahead.

- Voice-response dictation equipment with automatic transcription and printout on "ingenuous little machines that someday will be compatible with one or both of our others."

- Office layout, design, and full interior decorating with complete planning, including space-saving office modules that "will save us thousands!"
- Publication design, printing, promotion, storage, and fulfillment, "which really means that they do everything and just send us the checks at the end of every month" (which Jack thought might ease some growing anxiety he sensed around our otherwise rapt group).
- Library planning, staffing, and purchasing with a permanent 15 percent discount on all books and 110 periodicals, including new ones like *Sunbathers* and *Modern Photography* and oldies like *Collier's* and *Look*.

Mr. Wenski pointed out that *Collier's* and *Look* are defunct, but Jack replied, "Most of the companies at the course were using up some of their old brochures. Most of the equipment is out of date, too. But all the businessmen pointed out that nonprofits don't need the latest stuff." Mr. Colberg exploded, "I thought this was state-of-the-art." And Jack acknowledged, "I guess it's more like old art."

Sensing some apprehension, Jack interrupted his flow to indicate that if Our Organization buys the whole package, we will be listed in *Who's Who in American Purchasing,* which he said would help "put us on the map," adding: "We would be the only nonprofit in town that is even up to old art."

Gladys Pepper asked, "But will it really address our original purpose of improving performance?"

Jack responded, "Every single one of the companies promised that their changes alone will double our performance and all you have to do is multiply that by all the things I've mentioned and you'll see how much more efficient we'll be. Besides, I haven't even finished telling you what we could get."

Mrs. Greenlaw, head of our Public Relations Committee, interrupted, "Good gracious, can't you people smell the 'sizzle'? These days people want efficiency in their nonprofits, and we'll be miles ahead of the pack."

Even Mr. Gonzalez, who should have known better, was caught up in the prospect of efficiency and income potential. He and Mrs. Mitchell pointed out that we would be the only chapter in the country that would be seen on a par with the best of business corporations and that we could probably provide demonstrations to the other chapters and even sell them services and make a fortune. Mrs. Mitchell capped it: "Wouldn't we be at the top of National's list then!"

"We already are," exploded Mr. Zukert.

Mrs. Mitchell's "You know what I mean" ended the exchange.

Caught up in the optimism, Mr. Fales encouraged Jack to proceed, and Mr. Colberg was heard to mutter, "That's probably a good idea. I think he's going to hang himself this time."

Jack probably should have stopped while he had a fighting chance, but like many executive secretaries, if he knew when to stop, he didn't know how.

- A consortium of commercial galleries provides a monthly recycling of artwork, which keeps employees creative and happy. "Research shows that productivity is in direct correlation to the quantity, quality, and freshness of art. Organizations with monthly changes are twice as happy and one-third more creative."

Mr. Shapiro whispered to his neighbors, "Maybe we should get the daily service!"

Things were beginning to deteriorate, but Jack pressed on.

- Pets Incorporated provides a regular rotation of dogs and cats, aviaries, fish tanks, and reptile habitats. (Evidently this also increases productivity, which will probably be necessary considering Paula Masonowitz's ultimatum, "I'm not about to work in any crazy zoo!")

Jack struggled down to the wire with his final offering.

- There are now human resource development (HRD) services that work with us to develop, interpret, and administer job descriptions, salary scales, affirmative action plans, and the whole range of personnel policies, searches, and succession planning.

Out of curiosity, Mrs. Pepper asked, "What is succession planning?" Our leader, Mr. Russell, said he'd prefer to postpone consideration of that whole matter until the executive session.

"That's OK with me," Mrs. Pepper followed, "but let me ask another naive question. What exactly is an executive session?"

Mr. Colberg popped up, "The same as succession planning."

Having been on such a roller coaster of dreams and doubts and realizing that our Executive Secretary's report seemed to end as they usually did with a shaking of heads and tabling of action until the executive session, we prepared to take our break.

Just before we did, Mr. Shapiro asked if Jack by any chance had a dollar figure for what the package would cost. Jack stuttered out, "In the ballpark of something like forty-five thousand dollars, but that's their special rate for charities."

"Good Lord, that's more than our total annual income," exclaimed Mr. Zukert.

"I'm talking monthly," said Jack hoarsely.

"There goes 'sizzle,'" acknowledged Mrs. Greenlaw.

"And the reversal of our fortunes with National," said Mrs. Mitchell sadly.

"And another rejected report of our Task Force on Improved Performance," regretted Mr. Horton.

And with that, we took our break for punch and cookies.

After the break, Jack said that he needed authorization for the new Annual Report. Rev. Horsinger commented politely that he didn't recall having seen one for last year. Immediately Jack knew he had made a mistake. But he was too far into it to back out, so he blundered ahead: "We haven't finished the financials or the artwork, and the advertising agency that agreed to do the copy and layout on a volunteer basis got lucky and has some paid work, and the people at the Ajax Company haven't given us an answer yet as to whether they will print it when they've got some downtime on their press, but other than that, it's due out any day." Mrs. Pepper asked if it were reasonable to ask why we need a new one if we don't have an old one, and Jack explained that it was a new year, which Mrs. Pepper already knew. Neither quite knew what to say next.

Fortunately, Harriet Lortz moved the discussion ahead by suggesting that in the future we ought to have a lot more pictures, including shots of the Board in action. Mr. Colberg thought that might be hard to do. Mrs. Lortz persisted by saying that we all might take greater pride in the report and participate more fully in its distribution if the Directors were prominently featured in it. Mr. Colberg relented slightly, on the grounds that "it might at least spruce up our Board meetings." Mrs. O'Reilly said, "He should talk." She said people dressed better for Mass on a summer Sunday in Atlantic City than he ever did for a Board meeting. Then she grabbed him by the chin and, mimicking the advertisement, sang out, "Ring around the collar, ring around the collar!"

Mr. Russell suggested that we stay away from further comments on one another's persons, but Mrs. O'Reilly interjected that it was the only fun she got out of Board meetings anymore.

Mr. Wenski said he hoped that whenever we do another Annual Report, we should at least attempt to be different. He said that everybody's reports looked the same, and he made his point by asking us, "When was the last time we saw a nonprofit organization's Annual Report that didn't start with the Chairman's Report and then the Executive Secretary's Report? And we compound the problem by going one step worse and having a Founding Chairperson's Report that includes what must have been his high school graduation picture." Poor Mr. Henderson was obviously not ready for the blow. He was at first surprised, then hurt, then distressed—at which point he threw up his punch and cookies.

While several people rushed to his aid, young Beth Trister sat stunned. "I've never seen a person literally toss his cookies before," she said.

All this put a damper on further discussion about creative aspects of the Annual Report. Besides, someone figured that we have missed three years already and that if we wait another two, we could do a five-year wrap-up. Mrs. Buckminster said that she thought that made sense and that by then we may have enough to fill it up—to which Mr. Shapiro added, "And maybe a financial report that won't send us to jail!"

Mr. Fales reported for his Annual Meeting Committee. The Governor had been invited to speak, but so far no answer had been received. Because the day was getting closer, we needed to have a backup. Mrs. Greenlaw pointed out that this is exactly the same situation the organization has faced ten years in a row, and the Governor hasn't shown up yet. Mr. Knight pointed out that this year the Governor is a Republican. Mr. Scala wanted to know, "What the hell does that have to do with his showing up?" Mr. Knight said it was generally recognized that Republicans are more responsible. Mr. Russell reminded the group that we are nonpartisan.

When the group considered a substitute, just in case the Republican Governor didn't show up, it was obvious that we should turn once again to our Founder, who was persuaded to stand in for the Governor (it also improved his coloring and disposition). This would be the tenth year in a row that our community would have an opportunity to learn of the founding and earliest days of Our Organization. When discussion turned to an award for the speaker, Mr. Peter Paul Henderson discreetly left the room. In his absence, it was agreed that we would have the plaque made up for the Governor but ask Hardy's Sport Shop to be ready to switch the simulated brass plate on the award at the last minute.

In the absence of the Vice Chairperson, Mrs. Mitchell (who has missed five of the last eight meetings, eight of the last twelve, and twenty-one of the last thirty-two), Mr. Shapiro gave the report of the Personnel Committee.

The Board had referred to this committee the disagreement between the Executive Secretary and Mrs. Mitchell over who should approve sick leave. The Committee, recognizing that Mrs. Mitchell has had much more personnel experience than the Executive Secretary, recommended that all personnel decisions reside with her. Because of the sensitivity of the issue, the staff was asked to leave the room, and the Board quickly approved the Committee report. (While in executive session, the Board also voted to move the office, give a raise to "great old Paula," and revise the letterhead.)

The Committee also reported its position on maternity leave. It said that because the current staff members were all over forty, with the exception of Beverly, the one-day-a-week bookkeeper/dictaphone transcriber/telephone operator/general handyperson who had just had a baby, there was no need for a policy. The Board approved but said that should anyone get pregnant, the matter would be raised again. Mr. Zukert said that when the issue comes up again, the idea of coverage for paternity should also be considered. Mrs. O'Reilly snapped that if a man is involved in paternity, the association has no obligation whatsoever, and the matter was dropped.

All in all, it was not one of our better meetings.

Respectfully submitted,
Mrs. Jeffrey (Effie) Black,
Secretary of the Board of Directors

5

Minutes of
Our May
Board Meeting

The meeting began at 8:08 P.M.

Our Treasurer had, as instructed, submitted his written statements in advance of the meeting. Paula Masonowitz handed them out at the door. Before Mr. Shapiro could pounce, Mr. Gonzalez alerted the group that, as part of his report, he also wanted to discuss with the Board a letter we had received from the IRS. With perfect timing and stage presence, he left that hanging for a good eleven seconds and then pretended to start back to the financials. All the while, Paula Masonowitz, among whose duties is the role of Assistant Treasurer, shook her head sorrowfully from side to side.

Their ruse worked. As if on cue, Mr. Horton wanted to know, "What letter?"—and off we galloped with only

Mr. Colberg and Mr. Shapiro trying to rein us in with shouts of "Whoa there," "Hold up," and "Just a minute now," but they were dragged under the thundering stampede of IRS panic.

Mr. Gonzalez sat, staring at the letter, while the clamor rose to its crescendo and settled. At just the right moment, he raised the letter slightly and announced, in the tone he usually reserves for foreclosing mortgages, "They want proof that we're a public charity."

At first there was disbelief and cries of "What does this mean?" or, worse, "Does this mean what I think it does?"

Then confusion turned to defensiveness and rebuttal, like, "Who could be more needy than we are?"

Finally, logically, it evolved to the inevitable state of paranoia, with such normal reactions as "They're out to get us."

Gonzalez seemed to have rehearsed even this part of the drama. With hands in the air, he called for quiet, and just when we thought he was taking command of the situation, he announced, "I'm out . . . I quit." This was delivered in somewhat quaking but relatively level tones, quite unlike the outburst that followed: "Furthermore, you can count me out . . . forget it . . . who needs it . . . get yourself another boy . . . amscray . . . I can't take it another day . . . drop dead . . ." and miscellaneous other expressions rising to such a pitch that the last several were inaudible and probably just as well.

When calm was restored, Mr. Russell observed that in the face of the various expressions of reluctance and reservation, Mr. Gonzalez had won our sympathy. There was a round of applause, the first ever for our Treasurer.

Ms. Trister asked the obvious question: "What happens if we don't give the IRS a satisfactory answer?"

In funereal tones, Rev. Horsinger replied that we could lose our 501(c)(3). Mrs. O'Reilly said that she had never heard it called that before. Mr. Russell politely explained that the Reverend had not been speaking anatomically, and then everyone was confused. Know-it-all Mitchell said that losing one's 501(c)(3) means losing our tax exemption. This provided relief to most of the group, who obviously felt that this was by far the lesser of the two evils.

"So what does that mean?" persisted Mrs. O'Reilly.

"It means," said Mr. Gonzalez, "we're out . . . kaput . . . done . . . finished . . . back to square one . . ."

"OK, OK," intervened Mr. Russell, eager to avoid another of Harry's escalations.

Mrs. O'Reilly sorted it out this way: "As I understand it, it's taken all these years to work our way up to a 501(c) or whatever, and we could get shot all the way back to zero. What's wrong with starting back at one again, or couldn't we negotiate for a compromise and just go back to something in between, like 250(j)(11)?

Maybe our problem is that we got preoccupied with a false goal, like getting up to a 999(x)(32), and it would be good for us to get shaken up with a little loss of status. Life belongs to those who respond to setbacks and who pick themselves up off the floor and start climbing again with grit and determination."

Mr. Gonzalez realized that even a primer on the tax code would be wasted on someone whose next goal in life was to go from 501(c)(3) to become 501(c)(4), so he settled for explaining that without what we have now, people couldn't deduct their contributions to Our Organization.

In an understandable but totally unsuccessful effort to return us to another fiscal subject, Mr. Shapiro responded, "If I take our financial report seriously, that would affect very few people!"

"But it would affect all of us around this table," said Mr. Colberg.

"How come?" queried Mr. Widen.

"If you had ever given a nickel to this organization, you wouldn't have to ask," snapped Mr. Colberg.

Mr. Widen, hurt, explained, "At the office, I just check off the box that says 'United Way,' and they deduct for me."

"But it still comes out of your pay."

"The hell it does."

"Of course it does, and you haven't even been taking advantage of deducting it from your taxes, so the government has been keeping what it actually owed you."

Mr. Widen was crestfallen. "Isn't it awful suddenly to learn that the two groups you thought you could trust to do right by you, the United Way and the U. S. of A., have been in cahoots to take your money?"

Half of our group was unsettled to see a man so shattered, and the other half was shattered to see a man so unsettled.

We resolved the IRS issue by referring it to National.

Before moving on, Mr. Colberg wondered out loud how Gonzalez was going to top this performance next time to distract us from the financial report.

At that late point, Mr. Wenski arrived and explained that he had stopped to help a person with a dead battery, but because neither of them had jumper cables, they had to wait until someone else stopped who did.

Unruffled, our Chairperson reported for the Executive Committee. It had only met four times since our April gathering.

Mr. Russell said that the committee had covered a number of important items, some of which were so significant that he thought it best to ask the Board's blanket approval for what the committee had done and called on me as Secretary of both the Board and the Executive Committee to present a motion:

On behalf of the Executive Committee, it is moved and seconded to approve the actions of the Executive Committee at its April and May meetings.

Mr. Horton inquired, "I don't suppose it would do any good to ask what specific actions we're voting on, would it?"

"I'm afraid not," said Mr. Russell reluctantly. "You know the rules."

"I haven't been in a secret society since college," quipped Mrs. Pepper sarcastically. "Do you guys wear robes and call one another 'Brother Goblin'?"

Joining in what he thought was the merriment of her remark, Mr. Russell responded, "I guess that would make me the Grand Goblin," and he chuckled. Judging by Mrs. Pepper's stare of incredulous disbelief, it was clear that on at least this one occasion, Mr. Russell had misjudged his Board's mood.

Quick to recover, he used the pained silence to suggest that hearing no further discussion, he would call for action on the motion. I could catch only two or three barely discernible *ayes,* and Mr. Russell, sensing he was on shaky ground, wound down with a clever "Well, that should do it" and slipped into his Chairperson's report.

Later in the meeting, Mr. Colberg asked why the Executive Committee had not yet considered a budget for the next fiscal year, and it was explained that this was among the items we had voted on in adopting the Executive Committee report. A motion to adjourn taking precedence, the howls of Mr. Colberg, Mr. Shapiro, *et al.* were overridden.

In the absence of Mrs. Mitchell (who was excused for being out of town, but in a different town from the one that Mr. Zukert was excused for being in), Mr. Shapiro gave the report of the Personnel Committee, which had been asked to review the Association's fringe benefit program, which presently includes social security, worker's compensation, and unemployment insurance. At our last review, Mr. Yarborough said, "That sounds pretty generous to me," and the matter would have rested there. That was before the state convention, where some of our delegates heard that a lot of chapters provide basic health coverage and a few of the bigger ones even have a retirement plan. One chapter was viewed as being way out of line because it provides death and dismemberment insurance.

"Disgusting!" said Mrs. O'Reilly, but we weren't sure which of the extremes she was referring to.

Mr. Horton thought that all this sounded like the typical soft-hearted socialist behavior of nonprofit organizations, in which people should be willing to make a real sacrifice. Mrs. Workenthrader asked if his employer provided a good benefits package, and he responded, "Yes, but that is business, and besides, in business, where the bottom line is the name of the game, our necks are on the block twenty-four hours a day, every day, so there have to be some incentives."

Rev. Horsinger, moved to unnatural annoyance and apologizing that his children like to eat and that they sometimes get hurt and bleed, said that his church had actually begun to pay him (if collections warrant) and let him have basic health coverage. That did it. Right then and there the Personnel Committee was instructed to do its review.

At this meeting, Mr. Shapiro cleverly picked up where the first discussion had left off. "Ladies and gentlemen, our committee has taken its guidelines from the situation represented by the Reverend Horsinger . . ."

But before he could continue, Mr. Horton blurted out, "My God, we're going to buy Jack a house."

After careful study, the Committee recommended that our chapter provide basic health coverage, with a $250 deductible per episode, and that this be available to all people who have been on the staff for at least five years. As an extra benefit, the coverage can be extended to families as long as the employee pays the family share. Further, the Committee proposed that we go to a 50–50 co-payment plan on Major Medical, $5,000 deductible per episode, for persons who have been on the staff ten years or more and that for long-term employees a retirement plan be provided with the association matching the employee's contributions one to five as long as the whole sum is returned to the organization if the person doesn't stay until age seventy.

"Why that last part?" asked Ms. Trister.

"That's so the person is sure to stay till seventy," responded Mr. Shapiro.

With an eye on Jack, Mr. Colberg pleaded, "You haven't said enough about dismemberment."

Mindful not to incur Rev. Horsinger's wrath, Mr. Knight asked delicately if the Committee knew what this outlandish package might cost. Mr. Shapiro responded that the Committee knew that the Board wouldn't buy it all but had introduced it as an initial bargaining point and when the Board indicated what it might accept as a maximum, then prices would be secured and a fuller report would be presented to the Board. He said there was no rush because none of the staff was sick.

Further discussion revealed that the Board wanted the Committee to tone down some of the flashier coverage and bring in a recommendation with cost figures at a future meeting. Six amendments or substitutes to the motion for further study were defeated. Each would have required that in case coverage is voted, we would do it through a specific friend or firm. Unfortunately, all six proposals were different. Mr. Shapiro suggested that the final plan be submitted for bids, but those who had offered the motions made clear that most agents don't do business with nonprofits that way.

Mr. Russell asked if there were any further business from the Personnel Committee, and Mr. Shapiro said that the only other item was a dress code for the office, but because the absent Chairperson, Mrs. Mitchell, was so enthusiastic about this item, he preferred that it be left until she could be present. Paula Masonowitz crossed a trousered leg and glowered.

With considerable fanfare and apologies for past postponements, our Chairperson called on Mrs. Archer to give the report of the Program Committee, but she was so surprised actually to have a chance to give the report that she was unprepared. She said that she might be able to get her thoughts together if he could come back to her.

It should be noted that her lack of preparedness struck a blow to her ambitions to head the organization in the near future. Some had even thought she was in a

contest with Penelope Mitchell to replace Rodney Russell (though it should be noted that others saw it as a
three-woman race, there being another female officer
who should not be overlooked!).

While Mrs. Archer and Jack Neal began to huddle,
Mr. Russell asked if there were any shorter items we
could get out of the way. Ms. Trister reminded him that
we still had not taken up the recommendation of her
Bylaws Committee relating to whether the organization
should use the term *Chairman, Chairwoman, Chairperson,*
or *Chair.* But with the full support of the Board, Mr. Russell ruled that this could hardly be resolved with dispatch.

Mr. Russell mentioned that we had tabled an earlier
discussion about whether or not to combine the Public
Relations and Public Education committees and that
because this seemed like such an obvious move, he
thought we could slip it in now. Out of both corners of
his eyes, Mr. Russell saw the two rival Chairpersons
beginning to rise with nostrils flaring, teeth bared, and
eyes flashing, and said, "No, what I had in mind was
something easier."

Any doubts about the mistake he had made to open
the floor were sealed when Mrs. Lortz said that she
would like to reopen the proposal for an auxiliary. He
answered that we would wait for the Program Committee report with a break.

On reconvening, Mr. Russell asked Mrs. Archer if she
was now ready, and with her return to confidence and

positiveness she replied that it was a question of whether or not the Board was ready for a blockbuster of a report from the Program Committee. Clearly, Mrs. Archer had caught her breath. Jack Neal had scurried to dust off the flip chart, and the two were poised.

"To begin with," began Archer, "the organization needs a crisper, clearer, dynamic statement of mission. The one we've got now is strictly mush and doesn't do anything to position us at the starting gate with a sense of inspiration and energy. With apologies to the Public Relations Committee"—and from the look on Mrs. Greenlaw's face, more than apologies were needed— "we've gone outside the organization to get the advice of the very best PR/advertising/marketing minds in the community and can bring you their suggestion, which carries the unanimous recommendation of the full Program Committee."

And with a kind of singsong "Da-dah," she turned to Jack, who, on cue, flipped to the first page. Unfortunately, it had been so long since the presentation had been prepared that someone else had used the flip chart, and it was turned to this later entry:

STAFF NOTES ON BOARD REORGANIZATION
We Need:
More thinkers
More clout
More money
More doers

FULL OVERHAUL—and soon!
We need revolution, not evolution.

Jack, having flipped the chart, wasn't in a position to
see it, and thinking he had unveiled the crisper, clearer,
dynamic statement of mission, stood facing the Board,
beaming proudly. Gradually he realized something was
wrong, and at first he thought they didn't care for the
revised statement of mission, but something told him it
was worse than that. As eyes began to move from the display chart to him, he moved his eyes from them to the
display chart, and he decided that if there was a merciful
Lord, death would be instantaneous. Unfortunately, God
was otherwise occupied.

I'll say this for Jack—he doesn't give up easily. He
turned to the Board and, with absolutely the sickest grin
imaginable, stammered, "Just some scribbles from the staff
party." He might have gotten away with it, but his hands
were shaking so violently that when he tried to flip the
chart back to the correct pages, he sent them crashing to
the floor, display stand and all.

Perhaps symbolically, while he was down, Mr. Colberg suggested that this might be a good time for the
Board's own consideration of a revolution. Our Chairperson, ever fair, realizing that what Mr. Colberg had in
mind was more like an execution, suggested that we get
on with the Program Committee report and take up

other matters when cooler heads might prevail. "We don't want cool heads," shouted Mr. Shapiro, "We want his head."

By now Carol had gotten the stand righted and the charts flipped to the proper place, and Ms. Trister, who disliked confrontation anyway, picked the first quiet moment to observe, "I like it—I really like it," and all heads turned to figure out what she could possibly find to like. Embarrassed by the uncharacteristic attention, she just pointed to the proposed statement of mission, which was now on prominent display.

Perhaps because it required some thought, it tended to distract the group, even from murder. Rev. Horsinger, who understood that absorption with positive things can be calming and healing, was quick to pick up on Beth Trister's enthusiasm. "I think it's an absolute honey," he explained, and that unleashed a cacophony of "just great . . . a real winner . . . motivational as hell . . . brief but right on target," and so on.

Mrs. Archer didn't want to jar the group's enthusiasm by suggesting that they actually vote on such a major matter, so she interjected soothingly, "We're not asking you to vote on this tonight, but we want you to think about it and have it in mind as I present the rest of the report." And think about it we would. It was the first unifying theme in a long time and could be just what we need for harmony and thrust. For easy reference and in preparation for the big vote to come, here is the recommendation for our new mission statement:

> This community needs the good that Our Organization can do, so we should give it to them good.

Mrs. Archer explained to us that "like all good advertising, it doesn't present perfect grammar but it does grab, and in advertising, as everybody knows, grabber is more important than grammar."

Moving quickly, and with some return of confidence, Mrs. Archer said that her second point also picked up on the lessons of PR and marketing and involved (revealing the next page on her chart) SYNERGISM.

"We have to move out from and on to our mission in lockstep," she said, "as a common phalanx, as one cohort, integrating all of our activities and energies to maximize our opportunities and obligations meaningfully." Warming to her theme and its rapt reception, she added, "To put it another way, we should all be singing not just from the same hymn book but from the same page and stanza, and all our voices will rise in a harmonious thunder that will rock this community like it's never been rocked!"

Even Mrs. Greenlaw joined in the applause, but not without an audible aside: "Guess who wants to be the choirmaster!"

The report continued: "To make all this happen will require discipline, including hard choices on goals, hammering out measurable objectives, setting realistic timetables and budgets, and then using each of these Board meetings as a moment of truth to measure progress, including the evaluation of the performance of each and every Board member."

"That should get Jack his smaller Board," observed Mr. Scala. And some small cracks in the Board's enthusiasm began to appear.

Realizing that she was hitting pretty close to home and was in danger of losing her advantage, the Program Chairperson rushed ahead: "When we've put our own house in order, we'll be ready to move out to do the networking that is the secret of good community organization." Jack Neal peeked at the next page and, raising it inch by inch to double-check and then quintuple-check what it said, turned it over, but as he had for the past twenty minutes, he kept his face to the chart and away from the Board. At this point, he was looking at the word NETWORKING.

Mrs. Archer rushed on: "We need to build our bridges and influence with others who can help carry our load into every nook and cranny of this county. Our mistake is that we've been trying to go it alone, and no matter how good we are, the job is just too large. We need to enlist the support of service clubs, the PTA, student groups, women's organizations, auxiliaries, political organizations, fraternal lodges, and a host of other groups so that as they go about their activities, they will also be going about ours."

Mr. Fales sounded a note of caution, reminding us that we weren't altogether without experience at outreach. He recalled that Board members had once before taken assignments to meet with other organizations to spread the word and the load, but what had happened was that we got outmaneuvered and spent most of the next year fulfilling the resulting commitments to sell ten thousand raffle tickets for the Knights of Columbus, canvass the whole west side of town for the Cancer Society, handle six junior highs and nine elementary schools for National Firefighters Month, staff the fair booths for Amnesty International—and four of us are still learning sign language. "So much for networking," he concluded. "The wider we spread the net, the more work we get."

Mrs. Archer seized the initiative almost violently. "That's it!" she shouted. "That's exactly it! We've got to outsmart them, outwit them, outmaneuver them so that they end up doing our work, not the opposite."

"But shouldn't networking be a two-way street?" inquired Mr. Horton.

"Do you want to end up buying more jackets for the Little League?"

"I see your point."

"An evangelist goes out with zeal, passion, and conviction and comes back with sales of souls, not soles to sell."

Perhaps it was a bit of overkill, but to solidify her own sale, Mrs. Archer capped it all with "Whoever heard of a Mormon evangelist coming home a Catholic?"

Mrs. O'Reilly started to object, but the opposition's point was too well made to risk even a small protest.

Besides, Mrs. Archer was already into her point on networking.

"Once we've proved our conviction, tenacity, and influence, we'll be ready to go into the schools and churches." There were several gasps, and Rev. Horsinger looked half defensive and half fascinated. On the one hand, he didn't want anyone adding to his already difficult load, but on the other hand, he was curious how so many people did.

"What two groups really influence the behavior of our citizens as much as the schools and churches? We can make the case that concern for our cause is a matter of the whole person, and the whole person is what the schools and churches strive to develop. With enough pressure, we can take advantage of the natural guilt that good teachers and ministers carry around for all their charges who don't turn out perfect and, with their defenses down, convince them that adopting our cause might make the real difference. Why, we can even get the School Board to make our subject mandatory and get the Council of Churches to give at least a week and maybe even a month to our aspect of public service and personal growth."

Speaking from his own bias, Rev. Horsinger asked, was it not better "to leave it to the schools to teach fundamentals and the churches fundamentalism?"

Undeterred, Mrs. Archer came back with "It's a well-known fact that it's hard to get the attention of a hungry man."

The Reverend, beginning to feel outmaneuvered, shouted, "What the dickens does that have to do with what we're trying to do?"

But Archer closed with "People can just as easily be starved for love or culture or growth, and that's where we sneak in."

Sensing Rev. Horsinger's momentary helplessness, our Program Chairperson sprang to her last point and, like a conductor building toward the climax, snapped a pointed finger at Jack for the next chart. Having previously checked it out, he unfolded it with a flourish: WELL-DIRECTED SERVICES PRODUCE WELL-DESERVED INCOME.

If there had been any doubt about the Program Committee winning the day, it evaporated on that page.

The central and winning point was quite simply this: "There are a lot of people in this community who need what we've got, and we ought to give it best to those who are in a position to reward us. And here we're speaking of hundreds, if not thousands, of businesses in this community who are tired of giving to causes that are just doing good and don't have much proof of how much good they do and certainly don't do much good for the businesses making the contributions."

The usually skeptical Mr. Knight found himself responding spontaneously, "Here, here, it's about time someone realized that business responds to a quid pro quo." Pursuing a different tack, Mrs. Buckminster wondered if it wasn't the business of organizations like ours to serve those who can't afford help and to convince businesses that they should help, too.

"The name of the game is both," said Archer, leaving most of us a bit unnerved, but she won us back by pointing out that "if we do a good turn for businesses and they contribute lots of money to us for it, then we can increase our services to them and to others."

"The genius of it is mind-boggling," responded Mr. Wenski.

Mr. Knight almost finished the report for the Committee. "Instead of behaving like all these other whining charities with their hands out, we can go to businesses and offer them something they need, and who will they choose to give priority to when contribution time comes around? I'll tell you who. Our Organization."

For the second time that night, there was applause, but this time it was robust and prolonged.

Mr. Shapiro said that maybe we ought to combine the Program and Fundraising committees, which would have happened on the spot if the respected Rev. Horsinger hadn't said that perhaps that was premature.

In any case, Archer's stock had shot sky high, and the Board had momentarily forgotten Jack Neal's "Notes on Board Reorganization." There was a sense that at last we were on our way.

We had already covered so many momentous decisions that we didn't have any more time or energy to take up the executive session for evaluation of the Executive Secretary. For a while it looked as though a minority would filibuster until we did, but the crisis was averted when Mr. Russell promised that it would be a major part of our next meeting.

With that additional crisis passed, we adjourned at 11:37 P.M.

> *Respectfully submitted,*
> *Mrs. Jeffrey (Effie) Black,*
> *Secretary of the Board of Directors*

6

Notes from Our Annual Meeting (Our Big Fifteenth!) in June

In recognition of the special occasion, this year's Annual Meeting was held at Charlie's Bar and Grill rather than our usual location.

The dinner meeting was slow getting started because the reception itself was somewhat delayed. The problem was that we had agreed to charge $7.47, in keeping with our theme, "Getting a Fast Start on Our Next Fifteen Years," but the office had forgotten to bring change, and Charlie said it was bad practice to commingle his. Each person had to stand in line until we could give out the right change. Some people were willing to round it out at $7.50, which speeded things a little.

Though the delay seemed to upset a lot of people, it probably helped space things out because the bar arrangement presented its own backup. People had to stand in line to buy a drink ticket, then they had to stand in line to get their drink, and then they had to get in another line to turn in their ticket. It is against the house rules for the bartender to handle cash or tickets. Charlie is very careful.

People kept pointing out that the bulletin board downstairs announced that our meeting was scheduled for lunch rather than dinner. Mr. Scala commented, "Charlie must have heard how long our meetings go and planned accordingly." Mrs. Lortz proposed that we accept the announcement at face value and go home. Fortunately, we weren't formally assembled yet, so a motion wasn't in order.

It was when Jack Neal tried to get us to sit down that it became obvious that the microphone wasn't working. He stood there waving his hands, and people just waved back and got in line again.

It got our attention when Jack's twisting of the microphone produced such a piercing squeal that Mr. Gonzalez said, "It felt like having a lobotomy." Mr. Shapiro said he hadn't known that part of our Treasurer's past, but it helped in understanding our financial reports.

During the course of the meeting, Charlie came up twenty-seven times to adjust the microphone, and his percentages worked out to about one-third momentary success, one-third an even more penetrating screech, and one-third no sound at all, which turned out to be by far the preferred result.

In honor of the special anniversary, we had also secured the services of a professional master of ceremonies. He wasn't our first choice, and someone said he wasn't even on the initial list of 172 possibilities, but he was the one who agreed to do it, so we felt indebted. It turned out that the only thing appropriate about the choice was that he matched our screaming microphone.

"Doc" Haven is a disk jockey for WOCK, which he described as "strictly hard rock." He was introduced as "WOCK's Doc Jock," the host of "Crock of Rock," and with that he bounded to the microphone with such energy and shouting that we were more startled by him than by what he set the microphone to doing. Mr. Peter Paul Henderson, our Founder, First Chairperson, and Chairperson Emeritus, was seated at the place of honor next to the podium and reacted to Doc Jock as though he had just taken his first not-quite-conclusive jolt in the electric chair. He leaned back to get the full measure of this host of "Crock of Rock," and either because of the angle or the incomprehensibility of what he saw and heard, he just kept going until he disappeared behind the podium. At first only Mrs. Henderson noticed he was gone.

The brief interruption, which was prolonged a bit by Mr. Henderson's reluctance to leave his shelter, gave Doc Jock a chance to glance at the script, quite obviously for the first time. With Mr. Henderson shaking but hanging on beside him, our emcee called for the invocation by the person "who will be identified later." Unfortunately, either the committee or staff—at that point it didn't matter which—had forgotten to identify the invocator, but when that became obvious, our professional performer took it in stride: "With the authority vested in me as a former altar boy, I declare we've got God's zap." Rev. Horsinger was the only one to bow his head, but he seemed to be weeping or perhaps asking forgiveness.

Next on the script was a musical presentation by the seventh grade of Public School 17, which had been performing at a lot of public events since winning last December's Christmas Sing. The youngsters were wonderfully spirited as they marched in and took their practiced places according to sound and size. They had drawn their first breath for the opening note, but it became increasingly difficult to hold during the prolonged pause that followed. Ms. Florence Brady, the accompanist and director, didn't see a piano anywhere. Neither did anyone else. When called, Charlie explained that that was because there wasn't one upstairs and no one had bothered to ask him to move one in. For the sake of the kids, he said, he would arrange to turn off the TV in the bar, "which will get a lot of the regulars pretty steamed up," and Ms. Brady could use the upright that they had downstairs for their Saturday night "sing-alongs." It took a while for Charlie to gain the cooperation of people using the other meeting rooms and to quiet the protests of the regulars, but finally, if you strained, you could hear Ms. Brady pounding on the keys that worked, and with one of the older children filling in beautifully as choir-master, our entertainers did their medley of Christmas carols.

When they were finished, there was hearty applause. We could even hear the people down in the bar clapping and cheering, but Charlie told some of us later that that was because the TV was back on.

The host of "Crock of Rock" said he had a few announcements. The principal one was that the restrooms were out of order but alternatives had been planned for. "The men can use the Exxon station, which is to the right going out the front door, and the women can use Shell across the street."

Doc Jock said that while everyone was digging into the fruit cups, he would introduce the head table. He studied the script and lost some of his professional polish when he turned it on its side and then upside down and finally called Jack to help him sort it out, but it turned out that he wasn't very good at "stage left" and "stage right" and that some of the people had been switched around or hadn't shown up yet.

He began "on your left," and held up his left hand, and "on your right," and held up his right hand. "Let me begin with the person who 'will be identified later' and who gave us the invocation," he said.

From there it was all downhill. For the record, Mr. Russell is not Mrs. Mitchell, the mayor was not present, Jack Neal is not head of the Personnel Committee (though that might have been wishful thinking), the people on the left were actually on the right, and the ones announced as sitting closest to him were actually farthest away. The only person he got right was our Founder, who you may recall had attracted his attention earlier and was among the most eager not to be identified in any way by or with Doc Jock.

Our emcee was on a little safer ground when he said he wanted to acknowledge several special people seated out in the audience, but the result wasn't much better. It turned out not to matter that he so grossly mispronounced their names because after calling twenty-three names and waiting for each person to stand and be recognized, none of them were present, though one did come later.

It was about that time that we were startled to hear what sounded like the Fourth of July parade coming right through the room. Unfortunately, it was not to be that brief. The room next door had been rented out for a drum and bugle competition, and we were hearing just the first of thirty-three contending groups. We ate our fruit cups while someone sent for Charlie, but when he came up, he appeared to be straining to hear and, shouting over the din, announced, "I'm not sure I know what you mean, but I'll ask them to keep it a little quieter anyway."

That was the room to the right of us. It turned out that on the left, just cranking up, was the monthly meeting of the hard-of-hearing Toastmasters Club.

The mayor wasn't able to bring us personal greetings but had arranged to send a substitute, who eased our disappointment by assuring us that he was a blood relative on the mayor's wife's side and had been the mayor's driver since the day His Honor took office. Impressed with those credentials, we were complimented to learn so much of the family's history in this country and in Italy, Ireland, and Lithuania. Doc Jock had thoughtfully struck a lighter note when he smilingly announced to the group, "And that only includes relatives whose mothers and fathers were married," but the mayor's driver took it seriously and explained that "it wouldn't be right to mention the bastards because so many of them are still living."

Fortunately, he got to the Proclamation, which provided a reminder that most of those who are called on to read proclamations have not only not read them ahead of time but can't pronounce many of the words. Either proclamations are too scholarly for the people who read them, or the people who read them are too unschooled to handle them. There really ought to be a balance. Perhaps we should ask National to take this on as a service to the country.

By that point, we were aware of three things. One, it was going to be a very long evening; two, we were very hungry; and three, it was not to change film that the photographer had kept going down to the bar. At first we thought he was trying to take pictures at odd angles, but it became increasingly obvious that it was he who was at odd angles. As the mayor's kinsman/driver/representative was leaving, some of us thought the photographer was trying to catch a series of running pictures, but in fact he had simply started to lean to the left and the only way he could remain even partially upright was to move faster and faster in that direction. Unfortunately, as I think they say in sports, when he went down, he took someone out with him; even more unfortunately, it was the waitress carrying the tray with our salads topped with

Charlie's famous thick Russian dressing. This catastrophe was compounded when fifty-two salads with Charlie's famous thick Russian dressing landed on the United Way executive who had come to look us over. She (at least I think it was a she, it was hard to be sure at that point) seemed to take it with remarkably good spirits, though some said her laugh sounded a little hysterical. Mr. Zukert predicted that "she might not hold it totally against us. At least she got to go home early."

Charlie was more concerned about his waitress than about us and said, "He's your photographer, so don't blame me. And besides, those were all the salads we've got, so you'll just have to wait for the main course."

Food seemed a dim prospect when the waitress announced that she "wasn't going to work with that nutty group a minute longer," and Charlie said he'd go to the bar to see if anyone was in a condition to help out.

The only one not starving at this point was the new baby of our one-day-a-week bookkeeper/dictaphone transcriber/telephone operator/general handyperson, who had gotten so upset by the clamor that the only way to calm him was to breast-feed him a little ahead of schedule. Unfortunately, in the quiet that followed Charlie's announcement, people began to notice what was otherwise hardly noticeable, and the thing that became most noticeable was that we are not a very modern group. What was perhaps most noticeable of all was that once people noticed, they did everything possible not to notice, and all the not noticing and the efforts to avoid anyone else noticing added up to rather noticeably bizarre head movements. It was like fifty-two people watching fifty-two different doubles matches.

Fearing that Doc Jock would compound the shock with one of his observations or that Peter Paul Henderson would topple behind the podium again (most probably both), our Chairperson interceded and called for a break, thoughtfully reminding everyone about the Exxon and Shell stations.

No sooner had we reassembled with what seemed like the comforting prospect of food than a collective shriek began to build. It started with one or two people at one table and within seconds had spread to every table in the room. Some of us didn't comprehend, but those who did were aghast. Mrs. O'Reilly made it clear for all of us. With a sharper and higher pitch than even the microphone had yet reached, she announced that "what we are all looking at is pot roast," which frankly sounded and looked pretty good to me, but she coupled it with "and may the Lord forgive us, it's Good Friday." The moral issue we faced was as profound as a group could possibly grapple with together. Some said things like "God would certainly understand," and others countered with things like "We'll all be damned."

For all his insensitivity, Charlie demonstrated why he could run both the bar and the grill. Though we'd have to pay for it and he didn't have any on hand, he'd be willing to organize a group from the bar to get as many orders of fish and chips as we needed. It was an ideal solution, but we lost the better part of an hour while people made up their minds whether they would not eat pot roast as a gesture of symbolic support or would eat pot roast because they were starved and while we worked out the reimbursement that people would get because they weren't eating pot roast ("And shouldn't we get money back for the salads too?") and while we figured out how many wanted their fish and chips with ketchup and how many with vinegar. The dilemma involved in the symbolic protest was decided for most of us when the group agreed, by a vote of thirty to twenty-two, that the only people who could get reimbursed were those whose faith actually prohibited them from eating the pot roast. Symbolism is never very substantive anyway.

The next question was whether those who had the pot roast and were going to eat it should go ahead or wait until the others got their fish and chips. That vote was fairly decisive, so most of us ate while the others watched. They got back at us because the pot roast was terrible and we had to sit and watch them eat what looked like delicious fish and chips. Rev. Horsinger observed, "God works in mysterious ways." We were all thoughtful.

To make up for lost time, we moved right ahead with the Nominating Committee report. Mr. Russell explained that the Board elects its own officers, so the only role for the membership is to fill vacancies on the Board. On behalf of the Nominating Committee, Mr. Yarborough called for the reelection of all the current Board members and submitted three names for the vacancies. Two of those nominated were present but hadn't known they were being proposed, and both declined. Mrs. Plimpton had the good grace to say that her schedule just couldn't permit it, but Mr. Fleishman was overheard to say, "It's bad enough just coming to Annual Meetings." Speaking for the third nominee, an associate said, "There wasn't a chance in the world of his considering it." So we were back to the renominations.

Gloria Morrison asked if nominations could be made from the floor, but we all knew who she had in mind, and Mr. Yarborough alertly pointed out that nominations have to be made in advance. Mrs. Morrison noted, "Those two people didn't know in advance," but Mr. Yarborough said, "That's OK—the Nominating Committee knew."

When Mr. Yarborough asked for a vote on the reelections, Mrs. Morrison asked, "Do we have a policy on rotation and, if not, shouldn't we?" Mr. Peter Paul Henderson said he would be covering that in his address, which he didn't, but he carried the moment. Our loyal little band was reelected.

The master of ceremonies gave a big buildup to the next person: "It's now time to introduce the real leader of this organization, who will give us our marching orders not just for the next year but for the next fifteen years. And now I call on that person to come forward."

Unfortunately, Mr. Henderson, Mr. Russell, and Jack Neal all started for the podium at the very same instant, and when that became obvious to each of them, they froze in embarrassment and horror and might still be in that position even now if Doc Jock hadn't come to the rescue with "That's what I call teamwork. No wonder this organization has such depth of leadership. I think they all deserve a round of applause."

Out of relief that we had all survived a shared crisis, the applause was thunderous. It also saved our having to hear the usual reports of our Chairperson and Executive Secretary.

As planned, there was a break in the heavy business. With a deserved flourish and fanfare, the host of "Crock of Rock" introduced the winner of the AmVets Region 14 oratorical contest, "who at fifteen is clearly destined for national leadership." In ringing tones, the boy delivered his winning oration, "Without Wars, There Are No Heroes." It was hard to get back to business.

Mr. Russell took the chair at this point to call for committee reports. He reminded the eleven committee heads that each had been asked to limit presentations to no more than five minutes. Mrs. Archer came closest to the limit with eleven and a half minutes, and Mrs. Mitchell broke her own record of last year.

Charlie began coming up about every fifteen minutes to see if we were done yet, which made it a bit nerve-racking, but that was offset by having outlasted the drum and bugle competition.

Fortunately, the awards went fairly quickly. It became obvious that Jack Neal was not giving them to Doc Jock in the same order as Doc Jock was announcing them, and the swapping and confusion got a little complicated, along with trying to get people to agree to take the awards to most of the winners who weren't there anyway. Mr. Russell intervened again and asked everybody to turn in the awards distributed so far and assured everybody that they would be mailed to the proper people within a few days.

Mr. Colberg asked if we ever had executive sessions at Annual Meetings. Our master of ceremonies looked confused, so Mr. Russell said, "Don't worry about it, it's a little 'in' joke," but Jack Neal didn't laugh.

This brought us to the high point of the meeting, the address by our Founder, First Chairperson, and Chairperson Emeritus, who gave even the Region 14 winner a lesson in gilded oratory, along with a very detailed review of the history of Our Organization. For those who have minutes from any of the last nine Annual Meetings, you'll find a copy of pretty much the same address attached to them. For others, a copy of the annual address is available from the office.

As soon as Mr. Henderson finished, he was somewhat startled by the standing ovation, but it was clear that most people were using this as an excuse to move toward the door. Doc Jock stopped them in their tracks by reminding them that the state President was present to participate in this fifteenth anniversary and to make a surprise award. Geoffrey Mawby announced that in recognition of our Founder's extraordinary record of service, the state association was adding a seventy-eighth award to its list of special presentations made at each state convention.

The new award will be named for Peter Paul Henderson and will be given each year to the oldest person with the longest continuous record of service who was finally going off a chapter or state board. Some of us thought it was a mixed message, but the important thing was that Mr. Henderson thought it was wonderful.

It set us in the mood for the most serious item of business, the resolutions. None had been submitted in advance, but three came from the floor, two of which were serious and none of which was taken seriously. The first was from a Board member, of all people. Mr. Zukert submitted a proposal "that we not have Annual Meetings anymore." Charlie, though out of order as a nonmember, added an amendment "that at least you not have an Annual Meeting at Charlie's anymore." Mrs. Morrison suggested that we limit the terms of Board members and that the Nominating Committee be instructed to seek "new blood" to counter the "dry rot." Mr. Henderson winced, but we were not sure whether it was in response to the language or the substance.

The voice vote on Mrs. Morrison's resolution was challenged by Mrs. Morrison. The show of hands was not any more conclusive. The standing vote was questioned on the grounds that several people were simply stretching or leaving and we didn't have paper and pencils for a written vote. Beth Trister, though a newcomer, proved that she had learned her *Robert's Rules* by calling for a motion to adjourn. Mrs. Morrison said that was illegal. Charlie said we were all going to jail anyway if we didn't get out. We looked around and realized that other than Mrs. Morrison, the only ones left were Board members, so we agreed we'd reopen her resolution at the next

Board meeting. Mrs. Morrison saved us the trouble by concluding, "Don't bother."

Charlie usurped the authority of both the emcee and our Chairperson by announcing, "You are adjourned. And be sure to take your photographer with you." The photographer was the only one still smiling, but he probably didn't even know it.

We dragged him and ourselves out at 1:17 A.M.

Respectfully submitted,
Mrs. Jeffrey (Effie) Black,
Secretary of the Board of Directors

7

Minutes of Our Special Board Meeting in July (A Daytime Meeting!)

The meeting opened at 10:21 A.M.

We had waited an extra fifteen or twenty minutes for Mr. Peter Paul Henderson to arrive. Fearing the worst, Mr. Russell called Mrs. Henderson, who said that our Founding Chairperson had sprained his neck at the Annual Meeting and would have to miss his first meeting in fifteen years. She said that he thought about trying to make it, but both of them agreed it could jeopardize his suit against Our Organization.

Mr. Russell reported to everyone that Mr. Henderson was much better, which was good news by itself but also because it reduced the chances that the suit would involve death benefits.

We all agreed that it seemed strange not to have our Founder, First Chairperson, and Chairperson Emeritus at the table, and mostly nice things were said about him.

After everyone had said all the nice things they could think of and there was one of those long pauses you learn to recognize as preamble to what's really on people's minds, Mr. Scala said that maybe this was our one and only time to talk about how to get rid of him. For the next fifteen minutes, everyone's sentence began with something like "I know how much he has meant to the organization, but . . ." or "No one is more devoted to Mr. Henderson than I am, but . . . " or "I owe everything I've learned about this community to him, but . . ."

After a while, the prefaces changed to statements like "It looks like the old goat is going to live forever, so we'd better . . ." or "We may never have the chance again to get out from under that crazy dictator, so we'd better . . ." Finally people just let it all hang out, including every single one of the people who had opened the discussion with such praise. Left to cook long enough, toasts turn to roasts.

Mrs. Archer admitted that she dreaded having to sit beside him because "he seems to have only three ways of reacting to things. Depending on how strongly he feels, he scowls, shakes his head, or spits up."

Mr. Widen recalled "the time someone suggested we be willing to change our name to conform with

National's resolution and Mr. Henderson actually convulsed and Mr. McDonald had to give him CPR. That was really rough. Besides, McDonald has never been back."

Mr. Fales complained that Mr. Henderson always treated the organization like he owned it and made everybody else feel like an intruder. "He counters every suggestion he doesn't care for with something like 'The Founders would be aghast' or 'We who were there at the beginning never would have countenanced this' or, worst of all, 'We don't do it that way.'"

Mr. Yarborough agreed that it was difficult "having him always sitting there staring and disapproving. Hell, it's like having your grandfather propped up in your bedroom." Mrs. Workenthrader interjected, "If that had been your situation, you would never have had eleven kids."

For the rest of our discussion, it wasn't a question whether he should go but rather who would tell him. There has never been a more telling test whether an organization is made up of volunteers. When Mr. Russell suggested we draw straws, the tenor of the discussion switched back to sweetness and light, as twenty out of twenty-one withdrew themselves from consideration with such disqualifications as "He's been so good to me that I shouldn't be . . ." or "As his principal backer on the Board, I shouldn't be . . ." or "As one who roomed with him at the state convention, I shouldn't be . . ."

Mr. Widen said we could impose an attendance requirement and tell him he had fallen under the limit, but even our Founder's worst critics agreed that eighty-four out of eighty-five is not bad.

We thought we had hit on the solution when Mr. Knight suggested we get National to tell us that it is policy that everyone has to rotate off after six or eight years, but Mrs. Mitchell pointed out that half the National Board has been on thirty or more years, so that wouldn't work.

The next best thing was to vote to hire an objective outside independent management consultant who would give us strict advice that no person could serve more than ten consecutive years. Like binding arbitration, we would agree that we would have to accept the advice. Ms. Trister asked naively how we could be so sure that an objective outside independent consultant would reach that conclusion, and Mr. Horton responded disdainfully, "That's easy. You just hire one with that understanding."

Ms. Trister didn't want to challenge further Mr. Horton's worldliness, but without backing all the way down she asked, "What if our Founder, First Chairperson, and Chairperson Emeritus challenges the decision?" Mr. Russell responded with his own worldly observation: "We'll cross that bridge when we come to it."

The Board moved on with a new sense of both worldliness and independence.

With that necessity behind us, Mr. Russell reminded everybody that this was primarily a special meeting devoted to our financial crisis and the need to come up with immediate fundraising strategies.

Early on it was clear that our group prefers to think long range or at least that we thought an endowment could be built overnight because that's where we chose to start.

Mr. Zukert, Mrs. Buckminster, and others had recommended starting closer to the unpaid bills, but they were swimming upstream. It didn't take a vote to know that the overwhelming majority thought that an endowment had the right ring and seemed the best course for us.

"How much would we need?" asked Mr. Widen, and Mrs. Pepper countered, "It's silly to go through all this if we're going to worry about limits."

Our practical Banker and Treasurer, Mr. Gonzalez, laid out the starting points for our discussion. "The progression is (1) last year's income was $27,291.47, (2) projections for this year are $16,500, (3) our budget is $138,447.15, and so (4) our annual income from endowment should be at least $1 million."

Between cries of (1) "short-sightedness," (2) "pie in the sky," and (3) "whoa there," there was agreement that we were just at a talking stage and $1 million is a nice round figure to talk about.

That was the easy part. The next hurdle was how much of an endowment we'd need to "throw off a mil" (surely you recognize that this slang is not in keeping with your Secretary's literate reporting. I admit, though, that "throwing off a mil" conjures up an appealing image).

Between our Treasurer's call for a prudent 3 percent payout and the dreams of riches of the rest of us—and with a need to agree on a figure we could all calculate—we settled on 10 percent. The real problem was trying to figure out how much of an endowment we'd need to produce $1 million with annual payout at 10 percent. It wasn't that we couldn't have figured it out in our heads (or most of them); the problem was the sheer number of people who pulled out their little calculators, which all seemed to disagree. For at least twenty-five minutes we engaged in insulting exchanges on how to use a calculator but finally concluded that we were just dealing with another indication that some members of our group function on low batteries.

Easily the most unpleasant and unreasonable was our Treasurer, who said that over and over again, he and others at the bank had learned to trust their calculators rather than their minds and that therefore though logic would *seem* to serve up an answer of $10 million to produce $1 million at 10 percent, he had to accept the higher performance of his machine and therefore the answer was obviously $13,451,119.06.

There were five reactions:

1. "No wonder my mortgage is so high."
2. "I wouldn't trust their minds, either."
3. "Why don't we just do it on the blackboard like we did in high school?"
4. "What, and challenge the greatest technological development of the twentieth century?"
5. "God save us in this mechanical age!"

After further haggling, and in the name of team building and compromise, we agreed to take an average of the answers from our independent calculators, and so the minutes will show that to produce $1 million at 10 percent, we really need an endowment of $19,182,647.29 (actually, we used the mean and not the average because we left out the one extremely low figure of $90,000— the most popular number by far—and the high one of approximately $72 million.)

At that point, the Board felt that it had done its share and that the task should now be turned over to the best professional fundraiser in town as long as he could provide a satisfactory answer to the basic question, "How soon can he begin to send how much?"

Mr. Yarborough said that he hated to raise a possible problem, but he understood that the role of a fundraising consultant is to help *us* determine *our* development plan and guide *us* in getting *our* job done. There was percolating anger toward such shoddy professionalism.

Ever the compromiser, Mr. Scala said that the way around that attitude would be to "offer the fundraiser a percentage of everything he raises—that will get him off his duff."

The suspicious Mrs. O'Reilly queried, "What if he holds us up for a fifty-fifty split?"

Our Treasurer took a practical view: "We'd still end up with almost $10 million clear." But he almost spoiled it and the evening by having to add, "And that's not far from where my calculator came out."

Fortunately, our former Fundraising Chairman ignored the childishness and pointed out that if we need more than $19 million and if the fundraiser gets 50 percent, we'll actually have to raise closer to $40 million.

Almost to a person we agreed that that was the fundraiser's worry. "And besides," Mr. Wenski added, "why are we worrying? The consultant used to work for a foundation."

With that, a committee was appointed and authorized to negotiate arrangements.

Just in case our plan didn't work out and while we were on a roll, we took up the other likely gold mine involving bequests.

For this pot of gold, National already has a program that we can adopt and improve on. It's a "Bequest Cultivation Program," which involves getting lots of people to leave money to the organization in their wills.

There had been a national competition, involving some of the best advertising agencies, to name the effort and the winner was "Give as You Go." The runners-up had been "Expire Inspired," "Make Your Last Breath Last," and "God Can Count." There was a lot of support for the last one, but some people felt it was too subtle.

Some of the message is included in a TV spot we can get. An aging actor looks hard into the camera and delivers this grabber:

> God loves a cheerful giver,
> and God loves the poor;
> so approach the Judgment Day doubly blessed.

Mrs. Workenthrader observed that it would have been even better if after saying those words, the aged actor dropped dead.

Our Leader, Mr. Russell, said he found her comment morbid, but he also provided a hint that he had already been thinking about leaving us a little something. Noting his graying hair added pep to our consideration.

With a mixture of mounting enthusiasm and worry, Mrs. Mitchell asked, "What if National won't let us in on the project because we haven't paid past dues?"

"To be consistent, we'll let them have 50 percent of our take," responded Mr. Fales.

"I'll let the committee negotiate that, too," announced Mr. Russell.

In a rare display of unity, the board voted unanimously to "get lots of bequests right away and leave the implementation to the committee."

Ms. Trister added spirit to the promotion with this catchy summation:

> Make out a bequest
> To give as you go,
> Then face your long rest
> With a ho—ho-ho-ho.

Some of us thought this was so clever that maybe National would buy it in lieu of dues.

It was beginning to turn out to be true that fundraising can be fun.

At that point we thought of adjourning, but with the adrenaline running and some reminders of overdue bills, we decided to take just a short break and then devote our terrifically successful brainstorming to other streams of income.

During the break, an incident developed that might have cut into our positiveness. With poor timing, Jack Neal suggested that it might help our most immediate financial pressures if we agreed to pay for or at least make a donation toward our refreshments. This aroused latent tempers, but the gods were indeed with us this evening because we found ourselves thinking not about his petty and silly idea but about what is called "earned income." Indeed, we were so mobilized and interested that we found ourselves getting back into the agenda while still on our break. We even enthusiastically reconvened.

Right out of the box, someone mentioned a report from *Independent Sector* that says earned income is a current solution to the financial problems of many organizations.

At first there were some negative reactions, such as Mrs. Archer's suspicious "What do we have to do to earn it?" Mr. Fales carefully explained, "I hear the easiest way is to have a publication like a magazine that everyone wants to read and just produce it and sell it."

Picking up on that positive note, Mr. Knight added, "The best example is *National Geographic,* which they throw together from pictures they've already got in their files, and they earn about $500 million a year. Then they put a pittance of their earnings into some other products like films and books and the overall total zooms to a billion, almost all of it pure profit."

It might help put in perspective our exhilaration with this prospect to quote Mr. Scala, who spoke for all of us: "And we were setting our sights at only $20 million! Tell us more."

In just a matter of moments, these additional real-life examples were provided:

The Arthritis Foundation sells aspirin.

Zoos charge admission.

The Metropolitan Museum of Art sells fake art and umbrellas.

AAA pushes maps.

Elder Hostel sells opportunities to work in the jungle in summer.

Mrs. Archer indicated, "Some of these groups even have for-profit subsidiaries—that sounds neat." Reactions were enthusiastic until Mr. Knight retorted, "It would be hopeless for any nonprofit to be good enough to be a business, and besides, it would sully the image of free enterprise."

Rev. Horsinger reminded him that "businessmen are constantly telling nonprofits to be more like business," but Mr. Knight responded indignantly, "Of course they should aspire to be like businesses, but they should never compete or make a profit."

"What does that leave them?" asked Mrs. Archer.

"Hard-nosed charity," he snapped.

"What an oxymoron," observed Mrs. O'Reilly.

Undone in more ways than one, Archer shot back, "I am not."

That kind of give-and-take was bound to interfere with positive thoughts—and relationships. What had started out as a newly uncovered bonanza began to unravel. Any chance of revival was doomed with the next exchange.

"All we have to do is figure out what we've got that's worth selling and we're on our way," enthused Mr. Horton.

But our balloon was quickly deflated when Jack observed, "So far, we can't even give it away."

At that point a crash seemed inevitable, but we were saved by a reminder that the purpose of this evening's session was to think positively about our prospects and that despite some acknowledged obstacles, we could still become the comeback team of the '90s.

So we put behind us a preoccupation with lack of visible product, fuzzy image, and overall blandness and resolved to start afresh next time to crack the nut of earned income.

After all, any group that had already launched two multimillion-dollar efforts in one evening could afford a temporary setback and deserved a rest.

When Jack asked one last time what he should do with the bills, we answered in chorus, "Split them between the endowment and bequests, and don't get us back into such negative karma."

With that, this group of tired pathfinders, which had so effectively addressed its responsibilities to think big, decided to call it a day.

Respectfully submitted,
Mrs. Jeffrey (Effie) Black,
Secretary of the Board of Directors

8

Minutes of Our September Board Meeting

The meeting opened at 8:21 P.M. Our Founding Chairperson suggested that after the August break, maybe we should take turns and introduce ourselves and say where we're from. Everyone chuckled.

Mr. Scala asked if our bequest program was being implemented, and Jack Neal said that he had already started visiting funeral homes. Mr. Colberg questioned if it wasn't a little late for that, but Jack said he had gotten to it right after the July meeting. Mr. Colberg asked if we were going to have an executive session.

Mr. Russell announced that we would move right away to tackle the Treasurer's report. He even leavened the introduction with a bit of humor, though Mr. Gonzalez didn't see it that way: "It's always better," he said, "to attack the Treasurer than the staff." There was nervous laughter, particularly from Gonzalez and Jack.

Mr. Gonzalez held a different report in each hand, as though weighing their contents and a decision how to proceed. Mr. Colberg, suspecting another dodge, announced, "I'm not going to play eeny-meeny-miney-mo with you, Gonzalez. Let's get the bad news over with."

Unruffled, Mr. Gonzalez said, "I agree entirely that our time should be spent on the current figures, but I was just wondering if it wouldn't make sense to get the investment policies out of the way first. At the last meeting, with the prospect of a surge of income coming at us from several sources, you asked me to give thought to what we would do with all that income. It's really fairly straightforward, so perhaps I should get your nod on that and then go on to more immediate issues."

His timing and judgment were perfect once again. Before he had gotten halfway through the sentence, his handout was already on its way around the table, and knowing that most people were far more interested in investments than deficits, he had double momentum.

Though it may have been an empty gesture, he offered to quiet the protest by also distributing the hand-

out of the financial statements but was saved from it by
a chorus of "Oh no, let's get investments behind us first."

The recommendations were pretty straightforward:

Available Cash and Other Liquid Assets	Recommended Disposition
First $5,000	Assign to petty cash and put in non-interest-bearing checking account

Monthly Cash Flow Needs	Recommended Disposition
$5,000–$25,000	Non-interest-bearing checking account
$25,000–$50,000	Savings account (current yield, 1.7 percent)
$50,000–$100,000	Money market account (current yield, 2.1 percent)
$100,000–$500,000	Certificates of deposit (current yield, 2.6 percent)
Over $500,000	U.S. Treasury Bills (may be too risky)

After we had a chance to look this over but before
anyone could comment, Mr. Gonzalez reminded us that
as both our Banker and our Treasurer, he has a responsibility to recommend a prudent investment strategy, and
after pausing, he intoned that we, as trustees, must keep
in mind our fiduciary responsibilities. He ended by
reminding us of our earlier discussions and concerns
about legal liability. "And, of course, the greatest strength
and safety is to deal with a bank insured by the Federal
Deposit Insurance Corporation—the FDIC."

Ever alert and optimistic, Beth Trister jumped in with "What about sums that exceed the $100,000 FDIC limit?"

Most of us would have guessed that he could have gotten by with our usual "We'll cross that bridge when we come to it," but he won our confidence when he responded in candor, "I can arrange to spread the extra around."

Mr. Shapiro had done some quick figuring and judged that "if we had a million dollars, we'd probably be earning about 3¼ percent when we could be getting closer to 10 percent."

"Yes," shot back our Treasurer, "but you'd be sacrificing the strength and safety of a bank."

"I don't think you stated that quite accurately," snapped Shapiro. "We would be contributing to the strength and safety of a bank."

"Have it your way," sighed Gonzalez, "but I wouldn't want the responsibility of being Treasurer in an organization that blew a million dollars."

"It hasn't bothered you until now," observed Mr. Colberg.

"What other options do we have?" asked Mrs. Archer.

Mr. Gonzalez responded: "I suppose we could put it in a trunk and bury it," which brought a few smiles, but the matter was too serious for laughs.

Mr. Zukert said, "We could go for 'total return.'"

"I don't know what that is, but I like the sound of it," said Mrs. O'Reilly.

Mr. Zukert explained: "The concept allows you to invest in a combination of accounts, including common stocks, and to try to produce a predictable annual yield for current operations. In this way, you get the benefit of some of the income and also have a hedge against inflation."

It was clear that Mrs. O'Reilly didn't grasp the concept, but the idea of "total return" held enormous appeal, so she asked the Treasurer, "Who could be against our getting everything returned?"

"If you want it on your conscience that you've put public funds entrusted to you into common stocks, that's your business," warned Gonzalez, and it was obvious to everyone that he had immediately corralled the group toward his original proposal. Mrs. Mitchell spoke for the group: "I think we'd all be more comfortable if we followed the most careful, cautious, and conservative plan."

"We could take turns carrying it around in our shoes," cracked Mr. Scala.

"Knowing us, they would be open-toed," quipped Mrs. Pepper.

The matter was resolved for the interim by agreeing that we would use the early part of our windfall to deal with the deficit and then, as several chimed in, "We'll cross that bridge when we come to it."

Mrs. Mitchell asked if we shouldn't plan to pay off some of our past dues to National, and this momentarily struck a guilty chord that was quickly assuaged with an understanding that "when our reserves get above one quarter of a million, we'll try to negotiate our debt for ten cents on the dollar."

The always practical Rev. Horsinger asked if any of the money had begun flowing in yet, and Jack Neal responded, "We're beginning to see some signs." Mr. Colberg asked what that meant, and Jack responded, "Some dribs and drabs."

Mr. Shapiro persisted, "Could you be a bit more specific?"

Jack said, "This week we got a check for $25, a check for $10, a check for $5, and then a lot of little ones."

Mr. Colberg sighed, Mr. Shapiro cried, and Mr. Russell realized that there was no sense in getting any deeper into the current state of financial affairs. Not wanting to appear irresponsible, he concluded, "If things haven't turned around by November, we'll have to take a hard look."

With that sixty-day reprieve, even Mr. Gonzalez and Jack nodded agreement, and Mr. Russell picked up the pace.

Mr. Knight reported on our visit to a corporate chief executive officer (CEO). Throughout Mr. Knight's presentation, he was mindful of Mr. Horton's hurt feelings

when we had first talked about "getting some real corporate clout on our Board." As delicately as possible, Mr.
Knight reminded us that we had decided we should
strike for some high-level corporate CEO for the Board
with the expectation that he (why must they always use
he?) would bring swarms of his peers on too. Mr. Knight
continued, "In addition to getting his own participation,
we need to get that first corporation on board as a substantial contributor, and we need to crack its payroll
deduction, where the big bucks are. Also, once we get
those big boys with us, they do all kinds of other things
like help with printing, gifts of equipment, loaned executives, use of boardrooms"—"I'd like that," interjected
Mrs. Mitchell—"and all kinds of other things."

Mr. Knight said that the only way they had been able
to make the appointment was to assure the CEO that we
were not approaching him to be on our Board or to provide corporate support or to be part of his company's in-
plant solicitation or for any other tangible assistance but that
we just needed ten minutes of his time to get his advice.

With that, Mr. Knight seemed to stammer a bit,
causing Mr. Yarborough to ask, "Well, what were you
able to get?"

"We got twenty minutes."

"That's terrific, but what did he give us?"

"We got lots of good advice."

"Is that all?"

"By no means. We got our foot in the door, and that's about all we could expect on a first visit. Besides, he said that if his company's situation changes, he will surely let us know."

"What do you mean 'changes'?"

"Well, right now all the corporate executives are tied up with community responsibilities, with several commitments on line. In-plant solicitation is reserved for the United Way, but the CEO is pleased that we'll be part of that system and can participate in that way. He likes the idea of our doing services for companies and thinks that's a good way to win support, but he suggested that we start with some of the smaller companies first."

It was obvious that Mr. Knight was coming to another awkward juncture. Putting a good face on it, he added that the CEO said that "if it would help to have the deputy assistant Zone 17 sales manager on the Board, he'd broach the topic . . ."

No sooner was that out than the sullen Mr. Horton protested, "That lowly cricket isn't as high over there as I am in my company, and the CEO knows that."

Mr. Knight fumbled, "I'm afraid it was obvious that the CEO doesn't know you."

"That's absurd," protested Horton. "We were at the same ball once!"

The awkward silence was broken by Mrs. O'Reilly, who observed, "I guess you should have asked him to dance."

The deputy assistant Zone 17 sales manager was referred to the Nominating Committee.

Mrs. Workenthrader reported for her team, which had been assigned to visit the Voluntary Action Center (VAC). This part of the meeting also started well.

"I know that most of you are familiar with what the VAC does, but to bring us all up to speed, the Center helps recruit, train, and place volunteers in meaningful community assignments. It's kind of a broker between volunteers who are willing to give their time and the organizations that can use that time well."

That part sounded good to us, but the compact is a little more exacting than some of us figured.

"We met with the Director of the Center, who explained that the VAC has to be satisfied that an organization really is ready to use the volunteers effectively and to give them a sense of being part of the team in an important endeavor."

Mr. Fales picked up on the reporting: "It seems we can't just call over there for clerical help when we need it. They were quite definite that the Center is not running a 'Kelly Girls for Free' service."

Already our group was losing interest.

Ms. Trister was curious: "Well, what would the VAC do for us?"

Mrs. Workenthrader outlined: "If it is satisfied that we need volunteers for the good of our cause and have carefully thought through their orientation, training, and supervision, the VAC wants to work with us. It will also need assurances that its volunteers will be given opportunities for advancement and for the fullest use of their talents and experience in helping us build every aspect of the organization."

"I thought they were just volunteers," responded Mrs. O'Reilly.

"Sounds kind of pushy," added Mrs. Archer.

Mrs. Mitchell went on: "The VAC wanted me there as head of the Personnel Committee, though for the life of me I couldn't figure out why. It turns out they expect a work contract, job descriptions, evaluation procedures, and a lot of things we haven't gotten around to even for our staff."

"Sounds like they're not willing to do scut work anymore," said Mr. Yarborough.

"That doesn't seem to be it," replied Mrs. Workenthrader. "The Director assures us that the VAC's people are willing to dig in at every level of the organization, as long as they know it's important and feel that they are respected as individuals and as part of the team."

"When you come to think of it, that doesn't seem unreasonable," observed Rev. Horsinger.

"But they'd be getting more than the Board gets," replied Mrs. Lortz.

"Or the staff," added Jack.

After further discussion, a motion was passed "to thank the VAC for its time and interest but to indicate that at this stage Our Organization is not ready for volunteers."

While Mrs. Mitchell had the floor, she asked to continue with the Personnel Committee's report, which also dealt with the office move.

Mrs. Mitchell said that with the end of our one-year lease, it was time again to look for new quarters. Mr. Shapiro reacted, "Not again! Why in the world do we go through this what seems like every year?"

Mrs. Mitchell explained that "to get the best deal, we generally look for situations where someone has temporary space that they are willing to let us have at below-market cost. In the present case, the supermarket is ready to open its bakery department, so we have to move again."

Mr. Shapiro asked, "Wouldn't it make more sense to spend a little more and not use up so much of our energy with these constant moves?" But Mr. Zukert said he couldn't believe where this suggestion was coming from.

Mr. Shapiro defended himself by talking about "false economies," though he acknowledged that "any show of economy would be welcome around here."

Mrs. Mitchell admitted that her committee was badly split on the issue of whether to spend more and even whether to spend enough to get a location that would give us visibility and prestige.

"My God, I can hear Main Street coming next!" exclaimed Mr. Colberg.

"Well, as strange as that may seem, we actually have had that listed as one of our options," chimed in Mr. Fales, a member of the committee. "Some of us feel that maybe part of our problem is that we keep acting poor when maybe we should take off our hair shirt and strut a bit."

"You have to get your legs under you before you can strut," observed Mr. Shapiro profoundly.

For thirty minutes the Board went back and forth on the relative public relations of having the look of success as contrasted with the trappings of charity. Mrs. Greenlaw, commenting for the Public Relations Committee, provided a Solomon-like solution: "It should be right smack in the center of things for maximum visibility but semi-seedy so that people will want to help us."

"How about a tent on the Common?" offered Mr. Scala, and we all enjoyed the lighter moment, except

maybe the staff. Mrs. Archer said she heard that the
United Way may have some extra space, but several
Board members recoiled. They said that it was one thing
to belong to the United Way to get money from it and
quite another to give it the opportunity for complete
control. "We need our independence more than we need
the United Way's money," championed Mr. Widen, but
others seemed to be pondering where that logic led.

Some others inquired whether there might not be
some benefit in going in with several other organizations
to pool the rent so that there could be better space and
shared services. Jack Neal countered, "The disadvantage
with that is that a lot of small organizations get to take
advantage of all our know-how."

The pondering became more pondered.

Before we had resolved such matters as location and relative poverty, we found ourselves drawn into more everyday issues, such as furniture, equipment, and decorations.

"I don't care what we do as long as we get rid of
these crippling chairs," pleaded Mrs. O'Reilly. "And this
table, which keeps running my stockings," added Mrs.
Buckminster.

"And while we're on priorities, let's never again use
that sick green color on the walls. It's the one thing that
seems constant about our offices," said Mr. Yarborough.

"One of the Board members sold it to us by the
drum," said Jack, "and we weren't sure whether we

should give priority to conflict of interest or long-term commitment to sick green."

"Maybe that's why Mr. Henderson gets sick to his stomach," observed Ms. Trister.

"No, he was doing that before someone unloaded that paint on us," said Mrs. Lortz.

"Maybe it would help him and all of us if we had some windows next time," pleaded Rev. Horsinger.

"Next thing you know, you'll want stained glass, and we won't be able to see out anyway," grumbled Mr. Scala.

Windows led to curtains (Mrs. Archer thinks she has some old ones in the attic) and to other nice touches that would make it seem more homey. Concerns about cost were dispelled when the group volunteered to canvass garage sales for furniture and maybe even some good pictures and knickknacks.

Mr. Russell asked whether Mr. Knight thought that the CEO would be willing to donate some old furniture and equipment. Mr. Knight said that would be premature, but he indicated that his own office might have an old copier that at least was a little more modern than the thirteen-step, one-copy-at-a-time unit we have, for which the special paper is not made anymore.

Never one to leave a subject alone, Mr. Colberg added caustically, "Maybe that's why I never see financial reports anymore."

Despite some of the tone of our discussion, we found the group beginning to demonstrate both creativity and unity in dividing the tasks of finding or even donating old coffee machines, porch furniture, and wooden crates that could serve as file boxes.

Jack responded to several inquiries with assurances that he could provide receipts for fair-market value of such contributions, and the participation expanded considerably. (Personally, I can't wait to see that old desk from Mrs. Lortz's basement that is suddenly worth $300!)

Having planned for most of the details, it was agreed to leave to the Personnel Committee all other general arrangements for the move. The only final instructions reflected the general good feeling around the table and our overall optimism about the future because we instructed them to be sure to plan for expansion.

With the drums of sick green paint still in mind, Mrs. Buckminster asked what had become of our agreement to develop an ironclad conflict-of-interest policy. Mr. Yarborough apologized that he had not gotten to it but would get to work on it as long as it was understood that this wouldn't preclude his giving his wife, who is in the real estate business, an inside track "now that we're finally talking about real money for a good office." Mr. Horton also cautioned the Board "not to be too short-sighted because, after all, it's the Board members who know the organization's needs and are often in the best position to give us good deals."

"Like the green paint?" Mr. Scala inquired.

Mr. Horton's reaction was a perfect match to our current color scheme.

Mr. Widen said that for once maybe we could short-cut an item and just adopt a policy that said, like other organizations do, that any time an association does business with a Board member, the item should be put up for bid, and it should be agreed in advance that the Board member would match the lowest bid. In that way, the association gets the best price, the Board member gets the business, and there's no real conflict.

That was about to sail through until Mr. Zukert said he "had to confess that that's the way it works in most organizations, but if you really think about it, who's going to bother bidding if they know the Board member is going to get the business anyway?"

That was a lot to think about, but because it was, we slowed down on the conflict-of-interest proposal and asked Mr. Yarborough to keep at it.

And then it was a good moment to have a break.

After we came back, things still seemed good enough that Mr. Zukert took the chance of asking if he could reintroduce the idea of a Board retreat, and Mr. Russell warily gave a cautious go-ahead. Mr. Zukert explained that with so much money likely to be flowing in from bequests, the United Way, foundations, and maybe the sale of services and with the need to prepare ourselves for the new surge of money and increased expectations inherent in the Program Committee's report, perhaps the time was at hand for us to take a good block of time to think carefully about the state of the organization and its long-term development. To his astonishment, Harriet Lortz was the first to agree. Asked why she had such a change of heart, she responded, "First, after tonight's meeting, I'm feeling a bit more positive about things and even about people, so maybe it's worth the risk, but second, it's September and because I've been in that damn house with those damn kids this whole damn summer, I'll do anything to get away!"

For several minutes we busied ourselves with ideas for the agenda, costs ("Thank goodness we don't need to worry about that kind of thing anymore," chimed several members), what to wear, when to have it, and that old bugaboo, where to have it. In such a spirit of camaraderie, it was agreed that we would leave the location to our Chairperson and Mr. Zukert and then, as a liberated afterthought, to our Secretary also.

As to when, it was agreed that we ought not to put it off but should "strike while the iron is hot," "make hay," "seize the day," and such. So sometime in October—definitely before our next regular meeting—was agreed on.

We were about to adjourn when someone realized that Mr. Wenski had not arrived. We knew he would be confused if he came and found us not in session. It was agreed that I would pin a note on the door that would explain our adjournment and give him a chance to sign in so that he could get credit for attendance.

At that hour, and in that mood, almost no one seemed to want to bother with an executive session to evaluate the Executive Secretary. "Besides," said Mr. Scala resignedly, "you either like him or you don't, so what's to say?" Anyway, we all agreed that there would be plenty of informal opportunities to talk about people at the retreat. Jack said he thought he'd rather have our regular kangaroo court, but he wasn't taken seriously.

With that additional crisis past, we adjourned at 11:37 P.M.

> *Respectfully submitted,*
> *Mrs. Jeffrey (Effie) Black,*
> *Secretary of the Board of Directors*

9
Notes from Our Board Retreat in October

We had agreed that we would meet by 4:00 P.M. to beat the traffic for our bus trip to Camp Bluebird, which we had rented for the weekend from the YWCA. The last of our group (Mr. Wenski!) arrived at 4:46, but only minutes after several others who were also tardy. The circumstances allowed them to feel slightly less guilty because the rented school bus didn't arrive until 5:14 ("On Fridays, I have to wait until football practice is over," said the driver).

There were some problems along the way.

Mrs. Mitchell's seven pieces of designer luggage had to be placed on top of everyone else's so they wouldn't get damaged, but in the rickety old bus they kept falling off until we agreed we'd take turns holding them in our laps.

The bus had no springs, which may be all right for children who are prehemorrhoidal but made it difficult for our group.

There was an ugly moment when Mrs. Mitchell found out that Peter Paul Henderson was sitting on the bag he was supposed to be holding.

We weren't twenty minutes into our trip when it became obvious that the reason school buses are colored yellow is to blend with motion sickness.

Rev. Horsinger said that if he had ever known what the experience was like, he would never have backed busing. Mr. Horton summarized it for all of us: "It's no wonder these kids have scrambled brains."

Our problem was compounded by many wrong turns, too many navigators, frequent pit stops, and one long debate with a close vote on turning back.

Rodney Russell tried to lighten the situation by leading a sing-along, but it became obvious that the only song that everybody knew was "Row, Row, Row Your Boat," and after singing it eleven times and humming several others, we sat silent and sullen. Besides, on that jarring ride, it wasn't safe to unclench your teeth.

When it became obvious that the trip was going to be a great deal longer than its advertised hour and a half, Mr. Russell suggested that we use the time to advantage by beginning the evening's program with the orientation by our guest futurist, Waldo Wellington. Within moments, it was obvious it wouldn't work. At the first pothole, poor Mr. Wellington lost his uppers, and at the second, his head almost went through the roof. Shaken and glazed, he muttered about his own future and refused to go on.

To get off the defensive, the driver imposed the "stay-seated requirement" and forewarned us that if he heard any more guff, he would exercise his authority to require quiet also. The only person allowed to stand was Jack Neal, who by this time had the state map totally unfolded and with each turn adjusted the map for the changing direction. Our route became so twisting and Jack was gyrating the map so wildly that he sliced five Board members and came close to injuring several others. We voted to proceed on consensus, which may have prolonged the trip but saved a lot of blood that would have included a lot of Jack's.

We finally arrived at 9:15 P.M., but our jubilation was short-lived. The only light in Camp Bluebird was a stained yellow five-watt bulb at the entrance, which revealed a note we would rather not have found. It seemed that the caretaker/cook had given up on us and gone home:

> If you do get here, women are upstairs in Dolley Madison on the left, and men are downstairs in Martha Washington on the right.

Breakfast at 7:00–7:30 (no late arrivals served). Martha Washington's latrine is broken, so everybody should share Dolley Madison's.

At that moment, the fact that there was at least one latrine working provided some solace, but Mr. Russell faced his first decision and crisis. He tried a vote of hands of those who needed to go badly, but it came out seven women and seven men. While our Chairperson tried to figure out what to do next, the men headed for the woods, making the decision a great deal easier.

While we were thus occupied, the bus driver quietly unloaded our things. By the time we reassembled, he was already halfway up the hill, leaving us no choice but to stay. Our weary group of pilgrims huddled together, waiting for leadership.

Mr. Colberg snarled, "This is more like survival camp." Mr. Zukert added, "Like Outward Bound."

"Outward Bound is exactly what I was thinking of, too," said Mrs. Lortz.

Mr. Russell led the trudge to Martha Washington and Dolley Madison, respectively, and after setting up a schedule of male and female latrine watches, went into his dormitory, made up his cot, and pulled both the blanket and pillow over his head.

Some of us had worried that we might not wake up in time for the desperately needed but desperately brief breakfast. We needn't have worried. From 3:30 A.M. on, people began to crack out of the ice to test if they could still move. Not long after that, the lines outside the Dolley Madison latrine became long and unruly. The people on watch were swept aside by men and women who overnight had turned from uncivil to uncivilized. Mr. Russell rushed forward, still in his shorts, and though it was difficult to comprehend that this could be our leader, we kept our eyes on his face and not on his legs and tried to listen.

For a while it got terribly basic. We tried an alternation of boy, girl, boy, girl, but that didn't cover the situation adequately, so it came down to an interrogation of each person who was breaking through the lines, which went something like "How badly do you need to go?" and "How long do you think it will take you?"

Beyond that, there were some serious accusations that had to be worked through, such as the complaint that Mrs. Mitchell "sat in there and did her nails while the rest of us were in agony."

By this time it was already 7:15 and breakfast was half over, so Mr. Russell sent a delegation to negotiate with the caretaker/cook, who remained adamant that nothing would be served to anybody arriving after 7:30. We got around that by bringing trays to those still standing in line. These were errands of mercy that made us begin to feel warm, at least inside.

Breakfast was powdered eggs and bacon. Mr. Shapiro asked if any thought had been given to the dietary considerations of Jews in the group, and the caretaker/cook displayed momentary civility by offering to cook some sausage. He seemed hurt that his thoughtfulness was rebuffed, and he reverted to form.

There was no trouble getting people to the conference room on time, where a fire was being built. There was a stampede. Eight men and two women competed to build the best fire and were so quick about it that we already had an enormous blaze before it became obvious that the chimney was already stopped up with leaves. Each of us established his or her own endurance for how long the smoke could be tolerated while getting the benefit of the fire, but it wasn't long before all of us were back out in the cold, watching the smoke and thinking of liability.

As volunteers, we were enormously proud of how quickly the fire-and-rescue unit responded. These folks really saved both our necks and Camp Bluebird. When we asked them how they had gotten there so fast, they explained that the Y had told them what kind of group was going to be there for the weekend, and their total force was on alert.

We thanked them profusely, but it became obvious that was not quite the end of it. Though it seemed somewhat unvolunteerlike, they made no bones of the fact that they usually get a minimum of $100 for this kind of service, so we took a collection and they went off with about $135. Mr. Knight offered them an extra $15 if they would take him with them, but they just laughed, thinking he was kidding, and he cried, knowing he was not.

By then it was time for coffee and calisthenics, which seemed like a somewhat unusual combination. The reason became starkly obvious. It is absolutely necessary to keep that coffee moving through your system so that it doesn't have a chance to settle in any one place, particularly your stomach.

At 10:30 we met again in the conference room, with its stopped-up chimney and stomped-down fire. Mr. Fales thought he was being funny but was pretty much on the mark when he took a look at us and recited, "Give me . . . your huddled masses yearning to be free."

Out of politeness we stayed settled for Waldo Wellington's glimpse into the future:

Whenever we think about the future, it's generally defined as near-term, long-term, or the future generally. I like to talk about "forever."

In forever, there will be more of most things and many more of some. Though the growth rates will be uneven, by the time we reach even the first stages of forever, there will be more babies, more young people, more adults, and more females. There will not be as many males. Actually, there will be many fewer men for a long, long time. As women gain in dominance, they are likely to kill off most of the males. This will be the ultimate expression of liberation. Someday the pendulum may swing back, but not in the foreseeable forever.

Eighty-eight percent of the population will be beyond retirement age. There will be many more young old, old old, very old, and awfully old. In the farther reaches of forever, the terribly old will begin to disappear. Medical science will have reached the point that nobody will visibly die, but the oldest of the old will get so shriveled and shrunken that they will just get lost.

Social security will be taken out of the first $4 million of annual income, but benefits won't begin until age ninety. With cost-of-living adjustments compounded from now to forever, people will get $86,492 a month unless they have dependent children, in which case it will double. To support the aging population, child labor laws, a temporary fad of the twentieth century, will be repealed, and job training will be introduced as integral to neonatal parenting. The workweek will be back up to one hundred hours a week. The service economy will have given way to a slave economy.

I am sad to have to tell this particular group that volunteers will be considered enemies of the state. Anything that allows an individual to have personal influence on communities and societies will be considered antithetical to pure democracy, where everyone should have equal influence.

Research is already revealing that tolerance of even gradations of civility breeds unevenness in human behavior. In forever, everybody will be at their nastiest, which, despite its drawbacks, will mean that behavior will be far more predictable and life will be more on an even pace, albeit unbearable.

Sex-change operations and mind-altering drugs will have also contributed to a more egalitarian society. During the typical life span, people will have an average of two and three-eighths sex changes, and the state will administer periodic injections that will give everyone some sense of what it's like to be male, female, gay, straight, poor, rich, old, infantile, tubercular, fat, happy, dead, depressed, and average. It will be the only time in the history of the world when we will know for a fact who is actually average.

During incipient forever, we will already have instantaneous communication with everyone. What started with a megaphone and progressed through wireless radio and the TV and reached its break-through with the car phone will come to the point where any of us can press a button and speak to everybody everywhere. The ultimate attraction will be that nobody can not listen. Gradually, that will induce a catatonic state in an increasing portion of the population, but that gets us beyond forever and into the new creation.

We will no longer have the basic index, now called Gross Domestic Product—GDP. In its place, there will be AMW—All the Money in the World—but the object will still be the same, that is, each individual and nation will strive to get more of its share.

In the year 1995, what was then the United States had 18 percent of AMW, but by the year 2085, Mexico and its U.S. colony will be up to 23 percent.

The cost of carrying the U.S. debt will be the cause of the collapse of what is now known as the United States. Long before forever, the cost of paying for the debt will have reached 100 percent of income, and all other roles and services of government will have ceased. Civil libertarians will accept the blame for the government's going out of business, though they didn't plan it that way.

English will have been dropped as a second language, and even the Rockefellers and Mellons will have changed their names to Cortez and Hernandez so that their children will fit in.

Head Start will be part of prenatal care.

Right-to-Lifers will still picket the Supreme Court, but there will be a difference, because the Catholics and Pro-Choicers will have switched sides, which will be explained by the new old science of gradualism.

Trade deficits will set a new record.

Corporate mergers will have reduced us to one multinational conglomerate called G.O.D.

Israel's inflation rate will be at 112,784 percent, but the Jews and Arabs will have reached harmonious agreement on all issues except borders, arms, and God.

One of the best features beyond the horizon is that everybody will be a leader, except, of course, adult males, who will have disqualified themselves in the preforever. Women and young people will take their turns at being mayor, governor, president, and czar for a day, and congressional terms will be for a week with no one allowed to succeed herself.

Women, who were never really interested in the boring regular seasons of men's sports, will have reorganized things so that in pro sports there will be nothing but play-offs all year round. Everything and everyone will revolve around championship.

Perhaps one of the most encouraging prognostications for this group at this time is that through biofeedback, relaxation response, and other advanced forms of mind over matter, we will be able to control the temperatures of our bodies without regard to external climates.

Waldo tried to go on but was interrupted and engulfed by whistles, cheers, and shouts of "Bring on forever!"

With that as background, we thought about our own future, which some people calculated might not last the day. Mr. Russell tried to whip us into more positive thoughts. He had quite wisely postponed his plan to use this session to have us let it all hang out. He had looked around at those gaunt, taut, desperate faces and thought the time for absolute license should be put off.

Lunch had been scheduled as a cookout, but it didn't take too much pleading to convince our keeper to move it indoors. It really didn't make much difference. It would have been inedible either way. To get that little extra warmth, we had to sacrifice some of the benefit of the bird-watcher's lecture. The camp dining room had small windows, and every time he would see a bird, he'd shout something like "There's a nuthatch!" But within fifteen minutes, our necks had been snapped around so completely that we suffered from collective whiplash. Ms.

Trister said he wasn't very skilled anyway. He identified a robin as a cardinal, a turkey vulture as a seagull ("You can tell from the way he glides"), and a pileated wood-pecker as a great blue heron. Her doubts were cinched when she asked, "How many life birds do you have?" and he replied, "The ones that are flying or singing are all alive."

The lunch and program were followed by a nature walk, which might have been all right for young campers after the trails had been cleared of fall debris, but for us it was too dangerous to look up. In just half an hour we had a sprained ankle, a wrenched knee, a pulled groin, and a slipped disk, not to mention incipient poison ivy and oak. When the casualties were all counted, there was no escaping another emergency for the so-called volun-teer unit, and though it may not have seemed very car-ing, we asked the volunteers to hold their services under $100. Our first collection produced only $53.92, but Rev. Horsinger gave his Thanksgiving sermon early, and we collected just short of $91.

During our afternoon session, our Chairperson gam-bled by suggesting that we were ready for some blue-skying and asked people to speak their minds. We needed very little prodding.

"When will the other latrine be fixed?"

"How soon can we go home?"

"Let's draw straws to shoot the cook."

"Whose crazy idea was this?"

Looking at the positive side, Mr. Zukert, without reminding the group that it had been his idea, rationalized, "If part of the purpose of the retreat is to wrench us out of our everyday considerations, then we are already having a particularly successful experience."

Mr. Fales spoke for all of us: "Shoot him *and* the cook!"

Mr. Russell pleaded with us to try to relate the blue-skying to the organization, and there was an immediate response.

"Dissolve it," advised Mr. Shapiro. Mr. Russell chuckled, but the point got the first serious consideration of the day.

Encouraged that things were taking a positive turn, Mr. Russell pushed his luck: "What are some way-out things we should think about to make the Board more effective?" But he was careful to ignore Jack Neal's outstretched hand. That became a bit obvious and awkward because for at least three minutes, Jack's was the only hand raised, and for part of that time, he had both hands waving frantically.

Finally, Mrs. Workenthrader saved the moment, but hardly the retreat, by suggesting that maybe our Board meetings would be a bit more orderly and productive if, like at her DAR lodge, we sat by seniority, determined by office and years of service. She assured us this was just a "top-of-the-head kind of idea," but she produced a four-by-six-foot blueprint that showed everybody's place, including exact years of service. Most of us were impressed, but Mr. Zukert muttered, "If this idea is what she comes up with after months of preparation, it's terrible to think what she might really brainstorm." Mr. Fales warmed to the idea and took it a step further. "Maybe we could even get chairs with our names on the back that we get to keep."

"Next thing you know, someone will suggest we get jackets," snorted Mr. Colberg.

"Funny, I was just going to bring that up," said Mr. Widen.

For a moment it seemed that our brainstorming was spent but with nothing more substantial to latch onto, Mr. Yarborough picked up the thread and said that maybe we could be seated by some other pattern, like liberals and conservatives or our voting records.

"How 'bout the good guys on one side and the bad guys on the other?" asked Mr. Horton sarcastically.

Before Mr. Widen could get his reaction together, Mr. Colberg interjected, "Too lopsided," and we sat and thought for quite a while longer. No new thought presented itself, so Mrs. Greenlaw said that maybe we could put a person's chair back a place each time a meeting was missed.

"Except for the officers, of course," said Mrs. Mitchell, and even I had to agree with her.

That at least got us on a slightly different topic involving Board attendance requirements, which, because of my own strong support, seemed to become our first important agreement. Unfortunately, Mrs. Mitchell derailed it with a filibuster that began, "If you're going to attract the real community leaders, you'll have to accept that we can't be as available as the rest of you," and ended much later with "Quality is more important than quantity."

Mr. Zukert tried one last time by saying he "didn't mean to disagree with Mrs. Mitchell or to question the value of her very occasional participation," but he thought we should "not overlook the values of continuity and demonstrated dedication." Mrs. Mitchell skewered him with a reminder that "you were the one who assured the corporate CEO that he would never have to attend meetings."

"Oh, he would be different," offered Mr. Zukert, but though most of us might agree with him in practice, he lost this one on a rare adherence to principle. (It would have been different if the CEO had accepted.)

Wishing to salvage something from our clouded blue-skying, Mrs. Lortz suggested that we at least agree

that a person who comes in more than an hour late
shouldn't get credit for attendance. Mr. Knight reacted,
"You mean Wenski has never been here?" All being
aware that Wenski had no doubt gotten the message, the
matter was not pressed.

We moved to somewhat higher ground when Mrs.
Pepper asked if we could review the day of the week
scheduled for our meetings. As sometimes happens in
such gatherings, the unanticipated comment brought
the group alive, and for the next twenty minutes we
were vital and vibrant. From day of the week it went to
hour of the day, possible locations, whether meals
should be served, order of the agenda, shape of the
table, voting procedures, frequency of meetings, and
enough other offerings that every single person was
proposing, reacting, and interconnecting. Our retreat
was finally in gear.

Tempo and spirit continued to build until Mrs.
Mitchell, on behalf of the Personnel Committee, said that
in fairness to working women, we ought to consider
having the meetings on Saturday mornings ("Whose side
is she on anyway?" snapped Paula Masonowitz, not so
sotto voce). Mr. Shapiro reminded the group that Saturday was the Jewish sabbath, and while he had the floor
he pointed out that by holding rigidly to any one pattern, we would frequently schedule meetings on Jewish
holidays.

That set off Mrs. O'Reilly, who quickly gained the upper hand by an accusation that "you people of the Jewish persuasion want every other day, and when we Catholics and some other real Christians give in, you take advantage of us by plunking the Annual Meeting on the one day we ask for, and on top of that you serve pot roast on Good Friday . . ."

Seeing what an advantage she was gaining—and she was only just getting wound up—Mr. Shapiro thrust in, "I wasn't responsible, but I'm willing to be the first to apologize. Also, I'll submit once again, as I have for each of the last four years, a list of sixteen of the days we respectfully ask the Board to avoid. In addition, it seems reasonable to ask you to avoid our sabbath."

You could tell by the reactions that most of the group found Mr. Shapiro pretty convincing, but logic and fairness are never matches for hysteria.

Rev. Horsinger finally succeeded in getting the combatants into their corners and proposed that we all agree that other than an occasional special event, such as this retreat, we would avoid Saturdays and Sundays and any special holidays that are called to our attention by any member of the Board.

Mrs. O'Reilly tried to have the last word when she seemed to agree with the solution but had to add, "We've got saints you've never even heard of, and every blessed one of them has a day."

Mr. Shapiro was more gracious. "We'll miss you," he responded.

Mr. Russell called for a break.

Our caretaker/cook had prepared some painfully sour lemonade and then led us in vigorous calisthenics. Fortunately, the rescue unit was still there, and on a per capita basis, we were beginning to get our money's worth.

After the break, we were asked to think hard about our long-range plans. Mr. Russell began by suggesting that we review our current status and then consider where this might take us. "Before we know where we want to go, we have to know where we are now."

It was quickly apparent that even with the calisthenics and stomach pumping, the mood had turned cold.

Mr. Yarborough snapped, "You ask us where we are now and where we want to go? We're at the coldest, dampest, dreariest, most deserted camp in all of North America and maybe even the world. So that covers where we are. As to where we want to get to, my sights are focused on getting home, and I'm highly motivated to do that. The sooner the better! So that covers the future, if there is any hope of having one. What else do you want to talk about?"

Mr. Russell thought these comments somewhat negative, but he was wise enough not to take a vote. It was a small concession to avoid total mutiny when he said that we might shorten our Sunday morning session and that he'd try to get the bus here so that we could get an earlier start. It was something, but all in all he probably got only about as much credit as George Washington did when he said he'd stand while they crossed the Delaware to prove that he was a leader.

Ms. Trister said that she had an item left over from our discussion about the Board that could have some bearing on the future. She reminded the group, quite unnecessarily, that she was the newest and by far the youngest Board member (Mrs. Mitchell twitched) and said that she thought it would help us get along and do our collective job better "if Board meetings could be more interesting and stimulating, maybe even meaningful and fun."

The idea was so foreign that it was likely to hang out there and freeze, along with Beth Trister's enthusiasm, however naive. In grandmotherly fashion, Mrs. Buckminster explained that "serving on a Board is a lot like having a baby. The initial session involves anticipation and adventure, even if it doesn't live up to expectations, and all the rest simply ranges from nausea to cramps to pain, but it is what you produce that counts."

Ms. Trister and most of the rest of us were struck by that profound analogy.

Mr. Colberg spoiled the mood by observing, "So far, all we've done is lay an egg."

Mrs. Archer countered, "You men just don't understand, which is one of the reasons men don't make good Board members."

Mr. Russell reacted, "That seems a rather sweeping generalization."

Mrs. Archer got into it by adding that she "wished you'd let us run this place by ourselves for just six months."

Penelope Mitchell beamed.

Mr. Colberg said, "So moved."

We had to be reminded that we were just brainstorming.

Our Chairperson reminded us that our financial prospects seemed to be brightening.

"Assuming that things go well with our bequests, earned income, our applications to the United Way and the Cutting-Edge and Fail-Safe Foundation, and several other things that seem to be popping, let's daydream together about what we might do with all that money."

"Go to a Marriott," chimed in Mrs. Pepper.

"Burn a camp," offered Mr. Scala.

"Merge with a good organization," offered Mr. Horton.

"Get a real exec," slipped in Mr. Colberg.

"Now we're getting to it," observed Mr. Russell, referring to the growing participation, but Jack Neal, with a narrower orientation, paled.

"Get off probation," suggested Mrs. Mitchell.

"Pay off National," proposed Mr. Gonzalez.

"Go it alone so we could forget probation and the debt in one fell swoop," chimed in Mr. Widen.

As happens in such discussions, one or two thoughts triggered related observations, and that governs the flow of the discussion. In this case, we were back onto our old topic of "What do we get from National?" The litany that flowed from that question was not altogether positive. What we get are "cranky letters," "a lot of forms to fill out," and "a National meeting that costs an arm and a leg."

A few people were a bit more positive, reminding us, for example, that "we are part of an umbrella organization." Mr. Gonzalez suggested that "for those dues we could buy everybody a golden parachute."

"But we don't pay them anyway," scolded Mrs. Mitchell. Unfortunately she added, "And that leaves someone out in the cold." Her figure of speech did little to win her point.

Mr. Wenski reminded the group that we get the benefit of National's radio and TV coverage, but Mr. Fales responded, somewhat sarcastically, that he had to get up last Sunday morning about 3:45 A.M. for a Bromo Seltzer, and "while I was waiting for its effect, I turned on the TV and finally saw one of National's spots."

Mr. Horton pointed out, "We have to weigh the value of National presence and National leadership." But it was not quite clear which side he was on.

Rev. Horsinger said we needed to be fair and had to ask ourselves, "What do they get from keeping us in?"

In the long silence that followed, you could tell we recognized it was pretty much a standoff. That was usually where our discussions ended, except when we were considering repaying our debt.

Mrs. Workenthrader suggested, "While we're talking about money and willing to leave ourselves open by offering what might turn out to be crazy ideas, maybe all of us should commit ourselves to raising at least two or three thousand dollars this next year for something like a Program Development Fund for New Ventures." The group was both startled and silent, but when we recovered, the summary of the Board's reaction was that it was indeed a crazy idea and had put a crimp in anyone else's willingness to spout off the top of his or her head.

Mr. Widen, whose spout always seemed to be open anyway, asked the group to consider, "Why don't we form affiliates and make them pay us?" At first it seemed too crazy to talk about, but the more he went on, the more the idea appealed. "We could do what National does to State and State does to us. Instead of having the buck stop here, we can just pass it on to another layer."

It's a good lesson that you can never predict when and where the bright idea will emerge. How this had escaped us all these years was a bafflement. What we would do is organize subunits at the community and maybe even neighborhood levels and assign them their work with a requirement that they give us 25 percent of everything they raise.

"We could even impose standards and put them on probation," beamed Mr. Gonzalez.

"Won't the subunits expect a lot of services from us?" cautioned Mr. Colberg.

"We can just buck that on to State and National," chirped in Jack Neal, who was catching the spirit of it.

"And then the buck would stop at National," enthused Mr. Peter Paul Henderson, who was shaking with the delight of his evil thought.

"Maybe that's why they're setting up an international entity," observed Mrs. Mitchell.

The idea of going from a doer to an adviser, an imposer of standards and not a complier, a fund receiver and not a fundraiser gave us all such a sense of release that we felt spent but very good.

It was the right time to adjourn for our scheduled recreation.

Knowing his group by now, our caretaker/cook decided that volleyball, horseshoes, bird walks, and his other planned activities were all too dangerous. Yet he also realized that if we just sat around, we would freeze to death and he might be liable.

Ms. Trister proved the point that she was indeed the youngest when she suggested hopscotch and jumprope, which seemed ridiculously juvenile, but once we got into it, they were kind of fun and at least kept the blood circulating.

Mrs. Lortz and Mr. Yarborough swore it was an accident that Mr. Peter Paul Henderson's neck got caught in the jumprope. While he struggled, the knot seemed only to get tighter, and we debated whether it was worth calling the rescue unit for just one person. We decided it wasn't because we were just about out of money and if he didn't make it, we could try CPR and then call the rescuers if it didn't work because they usually got here in around ten minutes anyway.

Three of the more adventuresome souls did strike off for a hike, and after about a half hour we got worried and two others volunteered to be a search party. After another half hour, when none of the five had shown up, we agreed to whistle and yell as loud as we could so that they would know where home base was. After about six minutes of the most awful cacophony of blood-curdling screams, our friendly fire-and-rescue unit screeched in, and we knew it was time for a Saturday evening collection. Because we hadn't actually called the rescuers in, we suggested $25. They said that because five people were involved, it had to be at least $50. When we realized that that meant $10 a head, Mr. Zukert wanted to know, "Which five are they?" and, when told, refused to pay his fair share.

From old pants pockets, bottoms of purses, shoes, and even out of a bra or two, we scraped together $42.80, which the rescuers accepted and sped off on their errand of mercy.

It was remarkable that they were back in just twenty minutes with all five of our lost sheep safe, but sad to say, not sound. When we asked what had happened and how the rescuers had found our people so quickly, they said that it's routine on such Saturday night emergencies to go straight to Hardy's Tavern, which is not only what our original three had done but what the search party had duplicated, and by now all five looked sheepish and unsteady. The rule was that no liquor was allowed in the camp, but it was absolutely clear that our shifty-eyed little band had found a way to get around that. Even as horrified and humiliated as some of us felt, we could not help noticing how warm they looked.

One of the rescuers noticed that our Founder's head seemed to face backward and with our permission gave it a violent twist, which brought Mr. Henderson's eyes forward but not into focus. Two of us led him into the dining room.

The Y's promotional brochure said that Saturday night supper was "The Grand Splash," and if slop makes a splash, I suppose that's accurate.

We tried to make light of it by having a guessing game as to what the basic ingredients were, but the guesses that seemed to come closest only made the experience worse.

Several of us were hungry enough to try to gag the stuff down; it was like a family liver night ("Eat it or else!").

Ordinarily, I can survive by looking forward to dessert and coffee, but with breakfast and lunch in recent memory, I joined the gaggers.

After dinner, we joined together in the assembly room for a night of the kind of togetherness that forges a permanent bond among strangers.

Based on our experience on the bus, we decided to skip the scheduled sing-along, and based on this noon's lecture on birds, we decided to skip the young man's lecture on bark and moss. We went right to the one thing we had all been looking forward to this long day—the movies. At our last Board meeting, we had a prolonged discussion about what films to show and had found that the common denominator was cartoons.

While eleven people participated or advised in the setting up of the projector, the rest of us got the chairs unfolded and organized. These group activities absorbed about three-quarters of an hour, and just when we were ready to go, everyone noticed that Jack Neal had not set the screen up. It turned out that Jack had not set the screen up yet because Jack had forgotten the screen. The disappointment of older people is far greater than that of younger people when Saturday night's movies are taken away.

When no one came forward with a solution, Mr. Russell volunteered his bedsheet, and when he observed that such duty "might even warm it up," nineteen volunteers came forward. Once all nineteen sheets were pinned up, we could have had panoramic VistaVision.

When we were finally ready to go, Mr. Gonzalez turned off the lights with a flourish, which made it somewhat obvious that he also turned off all the power in the room. It took fifteen minutes to figure out that maybe we could unscrew most of the bulbs, and there was even some envy for those who burned their hands. At last we settled in for our cartoons. The first short ones were about Donald Duck and Woody Woodpecker and put us all in a better mood. We needed all the positive reserve we could muster for what came next.

In retrospect, we figured it had to be innocence that caused Jack to pick the full-length Felix, which he swore was listed as both a cartoon and an educational film. Had he looked just a little further, he would have found it listed more prominently as "Adult," "X," and "Hard Core."

With the two funny short subjects behind us, the conversation was chipper as we settled in for a whole forty-five minutes of Felix the Cat. What was funny was that it took us so long to figure out that it wasn't funny. One of the men admitted later that he knew in an instant what was coming but hadn't dared to admit he had already seen it. That's the opposite of courage.

It was obvious that night that self-fulfilling prophecy really does work. We were so prepared to be amused that the first time Felix mated, even Mrs. O'Reilly was laughing uproariously, and it wasn't until Felix began a ménage-à-trois that her howls turned to gasps, and either through an undersupply of oxygen or an oversupply of humiliation she passed out very cold. Each time we revived her, she came to only long enough to remember and went out again. We were scared enough about her that we called the volunteer fire-and-rescue squad. While waiting for its arrival, we prayed for Mrs. O'Reilly. We also prayed that her Medicare would cover the "contribution" and that our "volunteers" would accept an IOU.

When she was finally brought around long enough to stay around, we sat together like a stunned hunting party that had started out for rabbits and had encountered a herd of elephants. It was one of those moments in life when a whole group is literally, actually, truly, and in fact speechless. It was group shock.

The pall was finally broken by the one person who hadn't seemed to share in it. He was the same person who had seemed to share most deeply in the events of Hardy's Tavern. Mr. Wenski never changed that faraway grin until he finally realized the film had gone off and wasn't coming back on again.

Sunday breakfast was awful, and it wasn't just the food. No one looked at one another, which meant we had to look straight at the food, which was a cold lumpy oatmeal that looked back with a dare that few of us challenged. God willing, tonight we'd be home for real food.

To everyone's surprise, there was 100 percent attendance at our nondenominational service. With the events of the previous evening starkly with us, we prayed very hard. Jack Neal prayed hardest of all.

Rev. Horsinger spoke meaningfully on the evils of the flesh but said God was understanding of people who are exposed to sin against their wishes. He said it would only be a problem for those who looked even after they knew what they were looking at. Several prayed harder, and Mrs. O'Reilly wanted me to be specific about when she passed out.

When we began our last session, Mr. Colberg suggested that we begin with an executive session, but Rev. Horsinger reopened his sermon with emphasis on forgiveness, and when Jack bowed his head so low, some of us were fearful that too much blood would rush into it. Mr. Colberg said it would be the only time we could be sure something was in it.

Mr. Russell reminded the group that we had all been asked to read Brian O'Connell's *Board Member's Book* in preparation for the retreat and particularly for this session. He asked for reactions to the book. It was clear it was going to be a slow morning. Mr. Scala finally pointed out that he was slow getting to it and that when he started into it last night, he had fallen asleep before getting too far. Several others agreed that this had been their experience also. Mr. Zukert pointed out, in his wise way, that when people are that cold and miserable and have had such an upsetting experience, if any one book can put such a group to sleep, it must be considered a very valuable resource.

Mrs. Lortz said, "We ought to start every Board meeting with it."

Mr. Russell asked, "Is that all you got out of it?" and Mr. Yarborough seemed to speak for all of us when he responded, "So far."

Not getting far in that direction and feeling a little safer because the retreat was beginning to wind down, our Chairperson asked if any of us had any concerns we would want to bring up in this candid, safe atmosphere.

Mr. Fales expressed the concern that someone had used his toothbrush, which he had left in the latrine. Finally, Mr. Widen "fessed up" but offered the assurance that he had only used it as a nail brush.

Mrs. O'Reilly expressed concern about how she was going to confess the night's film experience, and Rev. Horsinger agreed to call Father Scallon to lay the groundwork. "Just one thing," she implored. "Don't tell him it happened at a retreat."

Mr. Horton stood to make a point, which drew our attention in this otherwise informal gathering. "Perhaps I'm the only one who can't take it, but I have to ask: Do we absolutely have to have lunch?" He gagged as he finished, and all around the room, shoulders hunched and shook in the same telltale retch. Jack Neal settled the matter by announcing, "It's already paid for." You can't argue with that, or at least I didn't think so.

Suddenly, Mr. Scala put a fist in the air and with rebellion in his eyes announced, "I can't do it, I won't do it, and even if we can't be reimbursed, we shouldn't put ourselves through it again!"

Mr. Gonzalez misread the uprising by commenting, "Didn't you hear what Jack said? It's already paid for."

Revolution swept the room. As unbelievable as it seemed, the Board was about to be independent and creative and not eat our caretaker/cook's Sunday lunch. The freedom from that action and the exhilaration of our boldness carried us to new heights. Mrs. Pepper even suggested we leave early and go to McDonald's.

The cheers were deafening—until we realized we had no money. Mr. Zukert suggested we try to borrow some from the fire-and-rescue volunteers. "They've got lots of it," he said. But nobody dared.

Finally, with initial hesitation but growing confidence, Penelope Mitchell stammered that she had withheld her mad money and asked, "Do you think fifty dollars would buy lunch?"

Some were surprised and hurt that she had held out on us, but I explained that with her personality, mad money is a pretty essential commodity. In any case, the news and realization that we were not going to have lunch here and had money to go to McDonald's and were leaving right away all lifted the group in rejoicing (and no doubt lifted Mrs. Mitchell's chances of being our next Chairperson).

The only item of business left was to call the rescue volunteers so they would know they had the rest of the weekend off. They said they'd wait until we were out of sight.

With all those decisions behind us and what was clearly a successful retreat under our belts, we packed and helped one another onto the bus and "row, row, rowed our boat" from Camp Bluebird toward McDonald's and home.

Respectfully submitted,
Mrs. Jeffrey (Effie) Black,
Secretary of the Board of Directors

10

Minutes of Our November Board Meeting

The meeting began almost on time at 8:09 P.M.
Mr. Russell acknowledged that the retreat had not
quite served the purpose of team building and camaraderie but thought we might rebuild some of our prior
togetherness if Mrs. Pepper would apologize to Mrs.
Archer and Mrs. Archer would apologize to Mr. Colberg
and Mr. Colberg would apologize to both Mrs. Greenlaw and Mr. Wenski and if Mrs. Greenlaw and Mr. Wenski would apologize to Rev. Horsinger and Mr. Fales,
respectively, and if Rev. Horsinger and Mr. Fales would
apologize to each other. The awkward nods across the
table with eyes averted from the object of one's contri-
tion would hardly be characterized as a foot-thumping
catharsis, but Mr. Russell took what he could get.

Reflecting on lessons from the retreat, Ms. Trister said that she has now attended an orientation session, six Board meetings, an Annual Meeting, and a Board retreat and had learned a lot about the other Board members and the founding of the organization, but "I have to confess that I am still not absolutely sure what the organization really does."

Mrs. O'Reilly responded reassuringly, "Not to worry dear, I've been here three years and I'm not sure, either. But it finally stops bothering you. You get caught up in the organization itself and just begin to ride with it."

We had agreed that for the first part of this November session, we would meet as a "committee of the whole" to discuss the possibility of broadening the Board to include more young people, seniors, persons of color, consumers, *women,* and other underrepresented groups, such as *women.*

A previous Board consideration of these topics had come up unexpectedly, and lacking the time to adapt to them, some misunderstandings occurred. Without mentioning names but to be somewhat specific, the following represent some of the reactions, followed by an indication of reactions to the reactions.

> "*I'm* under forty, and it's possible that someone else is also." ("If she represents our young blood, we should serve plasma rather than juice.")

"If diversity means more difference of opinion,
we can't stand it." ("What he can't stand is not
getting his own way as it is.")

"I can perfectly well represent the elder statesmen."
("If that means more of 'We've always done it
that way,' they're already overrepresented.")

"Consumers keep an organization close to the
grass roots." ("If we wanted to be a garden
club, we'd be a garden club.")

Because the foregoing is just a skimpy sample of our initial discussion, you'll understand why we felt we should
postpone fuller consideration until tempers and anxieties
cooled and why we didn't want to entrust such momentous matters to a committee.

Important as these issues are, we somehow managed
once again to get bogged down in procedural considerations. This started innocently enough (unless it was a
delaying tactic, which this particular person tries all the
time), with a question: "What exactly is a committee of
the whole, and what are its legal implications?"

Mr. Russell tried to be brief. "It's when the whole
Board serves at least temporarily as a committee so that it
behaves as a committee and not as a Board."

"That itself is encouraging," responded Mrs. Buckminster. "But could someone please answer my question?" Harriet Lortz volunteered, "A committee of the

whole is when we don't trust the Chairperson to appoint a good committee and/or when we don't trust anyone to represent our point of view and/or when we want to be present to see certain people squirm."

"That's very helpful, too," indicated Mrs. Buckminster, "but I still don't quite get why it's different from just having the Board take care of the issue without calling itself a committee of the whole."

Mr. Yarborough stepped in judiciously, and the two engaged in the following exchange.

"At its simplest, the Board acts like a large committee."

"Who does the committee report to?"

"The Board, of course."

"Why would the Board go through it twice?"

"The outcome might be entirely different."

"Who decides which time or which side was right?"

"The Board, of course."

"So I suppose we'd have to go through it still another time?"

"You've got it."

Our athletic couch potato, Alan Scala, quipped, "It comes down to the best two out of three."

Because almost all of us are used to watching at least championship events, we understood him perfectly, but still, most of us predicted that the losers would go for the best of seven.

That preliminary discussion seemed to have diverted us, but we agreed that it was a very useful experience that would prepare us to serve more effectively on this and other boards. We had all grown in the course of this discussion, and it felt good.

It wasn't long before we realized once again that we never seem to accumulate a layer of trust sufficient to protect us from crashing through to dissention and sniping. This was a perfect example.

We had agreed to begin this subject of broadening the Board with what we thought would be the easiest part, youth. To help give us a starting point, the Nominating Committee, which had agreed to offer up options and issues, suggested that we might be able to agree rather quickly to add a girl and a boy. That seemed obvious enough, but not to most of us. We got bogged down in defining *young,* and the bog turned into quicksand when we tried to separate the stages of youth and whether we were talking about children, young adults, or more of the younger types already on the Board who are somewhere between the mid-thirties and the mid-forties. Mr. Wenski tried to be cute: "As far as I can see—and I mean literally—I think I see only one of them." "But that doesn't include staff," insisted Paula Masonowitz.

With considerable agitation, Mrs. Lortz interrupted, "Why do we need any young squirts around here anyway? I come to meetings to get away from them!"

"For heaven's sake, Harriet, we're talking about people in their twenties and thirties."

"They're the very ones I want to get away from most."

At that stage, we took our first crack at trying to be specific about when youth ends. After endless debate, the only way to resolve it seemed to be by secret ballot. The answers ranged from thirty-five (I recognized Ms. Trister's penmanship) to sixty-five (I recognized the old geezer's handwriting, too). The average turned out to be forty-one and one-third, which we started to round off to forty, but Mrs. Greenlaw reacted violently (she must have just missed the cut).

In deference to her ballistic objections, we decided to come at the definition a little more broadly and with this approach defined *youth* as "not yet fully developed physically, intellectually, emotionally, and socially."

"If you leave out physically," said Mr. Fales, "it means we are already impressively and excessively young, so why don't we just leave it at that and go home?"

With his eye as usual on fundraising, Mr. Widen hinted, "We could even turn it to our advantage by pointing out on our applications how much even the Board is in need of development."

But aware that our new description wouldn't quite do for either our definition or our development, we turned once again to trying to separate the ages. As with our earlier attempts, I won't clutter the minutes by detailing the hourlong quarrel but will just provide a sampling of offerings and then our summary.

As indicated earlier, we agreed that before we could decide what is young, we had to decide who is not young, and that in turn led us to determine when, if ever, someone is safely labeled a "senior."

With admirable steering by our leader, we navigated this third shoot of the perilous rapids. We lost some people overboard but seemed to come out reasonably intact.

First of all, though there was a good deal of heartache and hurt feelings, we rejected age fifty as the end of youth.

At that point, some people felt rejected and others felt cornered, so it was much, much harder to consider even going below age forty-five. Someone suggested consulting with the Census Bureau and the Bureau of Labor Statistics, but possibly in full knowledge of what the outcome would be, Mrs. Pepper scoffed, "What do they know?"

In the end, with courage but with our majority thinning, we agreed that youth ends at forty-one and a third and that we should add to the Board people under forty-one and a third "as long as they are mature, stable, good credit risks, and they look older."

We also agreed we might even look for people who are in their mid-thirties if they are in positions of leadership, can provide substantial support, and are considered to have extraordinary judgment, sparkle, and vision.

Mr. Colberg observed, "On that basis, the average age of the current Board is about fifteen."

At that point, anyone would have assumed that deciding what and who is a senior would be by far our toughest hurdle, but we got over it in no time. At first, the special interests of several dictated that they had to propose something around seventy or seventy-five, and they probably never would have compromised except when Rev. Horsinger asked, "At what age do you and the others here think we should all be eligible for senior citizen discounts?" With that the tables turned completely. Indeed, if the merchants of the town had to be guided by this part of our discussion, they would all go broke. Forty-one and a third was about our average here also. However, because no one could argue for going straight from youth to senior status in one's early forties and everyone wanted to get senior discounts well before seventy, it was a snap to agree on "early sixties, certainly before sixty-five." So we settled on sixty-two and a half.

We hoped we were done with the seniors, but leaving some areas for subtleties is not our style. Mr. Widen wanted to know, "Even though we have established the ages of seniors, with everybody still so determined not to be identified this way (except for discounts!), how do you know who really is a senior?" Harriet Lortz said, "It turns out to be easier than you'd think. You just listen to see how people address them. If they're over sixty, people say, 'What can I do for you, dearie?' or 'How are you today, hon?'"

"OK," reacted Mr. Widen, "but how about those over seventy or even seventy-five?"

"That's even easier," responded Mrs. Lortz. "If they're over seventy-five, people just say, 'My, don't we look nice today!'"

So we had defined both seniors *and* youth, with an implied assumption that we had also pretty well taken care of middle age because that covered everybody else. Mrs. Workenthrader even tried to explain it as a syllogism: "We have defined the years of youth and seniors—ergo, we have defined middle age as in between—Q.E.D."

"Hold on," screamed Mrs. O'Reilly. "I'm not about to be flamboozled by such gibberish. Since when do you build a cellar and a roof and say you've got a house?"

Catching her point and showing her artistic bent, Mrs. Greenlaw said, "It's the same as painting a portrait below the waist and above the shoulders."

"Call it a Picasso for all I give a damn," begged Mr. Fales, "but please, can't we at least agree that what's in between is the middle?"

"What's that got to do with age?" countered Mrs. O'Reilly.

"I give up," retorted Fales.

"So it's agreed that we need to treat middle age with the seriousness we gave the other stages?" asked Mrs. Greenlaw of our Chairperson.

"Let's refer it to the Board," Mr. Russell decided wisely, and we all nodded approvingly.

Mr. Widen again tried to ease the tension with humor. He suggested that we might just use the definition he's heard that "middle age is when you are still willing to go anywhere and do anything as long as you're home in bed by 10:30," but though some of us smiled, most were too preoccupied with self-defense.

Though we never dared to put our age separations to a final vote, there at least didn't seem to be enough additional insults or personal privileges left in us to go on with it, so we decided to test our grids by placing ourselves in the appropriate categories to see where the voids and weaknesses might be.

When it became all too obvious that any even formal declarations were impossible of achievement, we finally agreed on a process that we all swore would go unchallenged, involve self-selection, allow no snickering, and provide reasonable degrees of fudging.

To achieve these ends, Chairman Russell simply asked us to arrange ourselves in three groups—youth on left, middle age in middle, and seniors on the right, and to ensure that our experiment wouldn't be influenced by social pressures, he asked us to try to do it with our eyes closed.

When there started to be protests, he asked the group to think of this as just another kind of "straw vote" and reminded us that we were just functioning as a committee of the whole.

Perhaps we were just tired of the subject, but whatever the reason, we were surprisingly docile and, at the count of three, closed our eyes and fumbled toward our proper places.

Jack and Paula, as staff, didn't need to keep their eyes closed and were able to see what this maneuver looked like. To be sure he wasn't overheard, Jack scribbled a note to Paula, which he later left on the table and I intercepted for the record (it should always be as complete as possible!):

> They're behaving in an absolute caricature of themselves.
>
> They're obviously lost. As usual, they're without vision. Look at them stumbling, groping, pushing, and shoving.
>
> Listen to the lewd asides.

> They don't know their right from their left and, as
> usual, are moving in the wrong direction.
> It is a classic microcosm of our Board in action.
> Eat this note.

When we opened our eyes and shuffled closer to our appropriate places, we were more or less where we belonged.

Accepting the prohibition not to mention names, it's fair to report that there were three people who declared themselves as young (one of whom is older than I am and another I thought might turn up on the far right), almost all of us were in the middle (which means there was about an equal balance of truth and fudge), and there was our Founder, Peter Paul Henderson, alone on the right.

Looking at our groupings, Mrs. Workenthrader observed, "Perhaps we started in the wrong place. It's obvious we are lacking in seniors." Mr. Henderson, furious and hurt, retorted, "I have two things to say to you children. First, it takes only one elder statesman to represent wisdom, and second, experienced people know that when the chips are down, you don't count heads, you weigh them."

There was a cogent pause before Mr. Colberg beat others to point out that "If that's the case, we are in double jeopardy."

"Yeah," added Wenski, "three strikes and you're out."

"Throw him another ball," urged Shapiro.

Despite our Founder's protests and with a wonderful feeling of liberation, we ended our consideration of youth with a decision to focus on seniors the next time. We also agreed to keep an open mind to considering "a real girl and boy, not for what they can do for us but for what we can do for them." Mrs. O'Reilly cooed, "That will be an extra service to the community by Our Organization."

Mr. Knight was somewhat less optimistic: "We'll probably all be jailed for contributing to the delinquency of minors."

Before we could break, Mr. Fales asked when we would report for the committee of the whole to the full Board. "All in good time," we agreed, "all in good time."

And with that we took our break.

There had been a previous telephone vote authorizing us to join in the Forum of Voluntary Agencies' protest against a proposed City Council ordinance that would restrict public demonstrations to protests that are licensed and cleared by the City Council and that provide at least six months' notice. In no case would protests of more than fifteen people be allowed during working hours or on weekends or holidays. It would also make it illegal for voluntary organizations that receive government funds in any form or might anticipate applying for government funds in any form to make any contacts with any government agencies or officials.

Our discussion began with questions and complaints about whether we should have given our OK without full preparation and formal discussion. For example, Mrs. Archer protested that the Forum could have waited until all of the organizations had taken it up at their regular meetings. "I didn't even know what Jack was talking about on the phone," she said. (Mr. Zukert whispered to his neighbor that Mrs. Archer wouldn't have understood it even if Jack had written it or said it in person. I couldn't decide whether he was disparaging Jack's articulateness or Mrs. Archer's comprehension or both.)

Mr. Horton pointed out that it would have taken six months or more to get all those approvals, "and by then the ordinances would have passed," but Mrs. Mitchell insisted that "process is always more important than speed, and what's the rush anyway? The Forum is making a federal case out of some silly regulations."

After at least fifteen minutes of prolonged discussion about the process and timetable of our decision, we agreed to move to discussion of other aspects of the matter, and if our conclusions called for it, we would ask the Forum to rescind our participation in last week's City Council session.

It would probably have been easier and more amenable to positive relationships if we had stayed with our upset with the Forum's process, for we quickly found ourselves in a nasty argument about whether we should get involved with government under any circumstances. "It's unseemly and certainly doesn't fit our responsibility to be independent," posited Mr. Fales.

"Precisely," pontificated Founder Henderson, "and that's why our Charter prohibits it."

Off balance and a bit bewildered, Mr. Smucker, the new Chairperson of our Community Relations Committee, indicated that "we've studied your fifty-three-page bylaws and have fine-combed a hundred and sixteen pages of policies and weren't able to find one word relating or not relating to government and . . ."

"Precisely," interrupted Founder Henderson, "and that was deliberate. We wanted no misunderstanding, no loopholes, and no possibility of amendment." Before his blood pressure choked him off, he ended with a scolding, "And let me tell you, young man, that if any crazy political pinko causes us to get in bed with government, we'd deserve to lose our support, our reputation, and our Charter." Red-faced and rubber-kneed, he slumped into his seat and gasped for breath.

For a while, all was still.

Finally, slowly and judiciously, Mr. Smucker resumed his report. "I, too, am concerned about retaining our Charter"—we all noted that he didn't include the matters of support and reputation—"but I don't think a careful or even casual review of the law can suggest to anybody that we can't deal with government. Indeed, it's because of just such a threat to our right to work with government that we're involved with this proposed ordinance."

Being wound up but not winding down, Mr. Smucker added, "Why did you appoint a Community Relations Committee and ask me to chair the blessed thing if you didn't intend to relate in any way to this community's government?"

Chairperson Russell tried to clarify the issues before calling on any one of the eleven persons who had their hands up. "In fairness, my good friend and colleague Mr. Smucker"—we recognized this as the quiet prelude to a quick pounce—"I don't think we interpreted that 'community' necessarily includes government. I really suppose we were thinking more of people and organizations."

"That's absolutely right," snapped Mrs. O'Reilly.

"Precisely," gurgled our Founder.

"And secondly," soothed Mr. Russell, "though your point may have merit that there may be times, for example, out of self-protection, when we must deal with government, we need to be extremely careful about dealing with those people."

Before the sputtering Mr. Smucker could form real words, Mr. Russell opened it up to the rest of us.

"There are three distinct spheres of society," lectured Mr. Horton. "Well, there are actually four if you want to include the media. . . ." ("Oh, my God," exploded Mrs. O'Reilly, "let's not muddy the discussion and ourselves with them.") "The three spheres," continued Mr. Horton, "are the commercial, governmental, and independent sectors. Like the branches of government—executive, legislative, and judicial—the three spheres are separate, but unlike the three branches of government, they are not equal. Throughout our history, we have come to recognize that the values and success of America depend on business, voluntary organizations, and government, in that order, and therefore it is essential to retain the separateness of the three sectors and even more essential not to dilute the preciousness of the first two by sullying them with politics and politicians."

Mr. Horton concluded his incisive exposition: "That is why I supported the effort to protect our independence from the City Council and why I abhor any interpretation that such action establishes any precedence for working otherwise with government."

Mr. Russell responded for almost all of us when he rose and toasted, "Mr. Horton, brilliantly put. Spoken with the wisdom of Jefferson and the eloquence of Adams."

Despite Mr. Smucker's murmured "The Forefathers would have been appalled," the hands had disappeared. Mr. Smucker had had his say, and the sense of the meeting could be summarized clearly and proudly that we believe in separation and independence. Hurrah!

With that we turned to the substance of the matter (always the boring part) and talked about the proposed resolutions on demonstrations, specifically beginning with the clearance procedures and timetable, and the prohibitions of any such actions during business hours, weekends, and holidays.

"Maybe the six months' notice could be reduced to three or four," said Mrs. Lortz compromisingly. "Less than that and everybody would be surprised."

Mr. Smucker just held his despairing head in his hands and let it pass, which it did and by vote.

On the second issue, involving who should be able to receive government funds and still be free to communicate with government, Mr. Smucker began to lift up, with fight in his frightened eyes and a stance of defiant posture. Some of us could picture Don Quixote or General Custer, outnumbered and overwhelmed, and we were almost as sure his fate would be the same as theirs.

Fortunately, Mr. Smucker's goodness and ferocity backed off the warriors. Besides, it was obvious we prob-

ably had a standoff between those who thought that if
you took handouts from government, you should be dis-
enfranchised and those who wanted the handouts as long
as government stays off our backs.

We found we were getting into some very deep
water involving very deep feelings about such deep issues
as who deserves welfare ("Cheats should be prosecuted,"
"Right on!"), entitlements ("We aren't talking about
social security, are we?" "Damn right we are!" "I've
changed my mind—forgive me, AARP"), government
employees' being useless bureaucrats ("Not all of them,"
"My wife's a cop," "That's one vote for Smucker"), and
independent research laboratories ("They're already
independent," "But we want them at least to talk to government about health policy," "I'm in, Mr. Smucker").

And that was the trend and the landslide. We voted
on the spot against disenfranchisement.

So swift was our reversal and action that Mr.
Smucker was still standing, flailing his imaginary sword,
when someone got through to him that he had won, and
when absolutely assured, he accepted help into his seat
and put his head back into his hands and this time wept
with relief and joy.

To leave him at peace, we asked our Executive Secretary how the City Council was leaning, and he said it
looked rocky. With that our antigovernment, anti-

involvement cohort of isolationists got aroused to get involved and voted to be totally engaged with the Forum of Voluntary Agencies crusade.

At that point, we looked over to see that Mr. Smucker had his head in his hands and was weeping and nodding and that our Founder had his weeping head in his hands but was shaking it the other way. They were still slumped over next to each other, nodding or shaking and weeping.

It was a profound lesson in life. There are winners and losers; who is up is down; fortunes change in an instant; right wins over might—and it all happened right there before our very eyes at a meeting of Our Organization.

With tears in our own eyes, we decided on a stretch.

Our final subject involved the report of our Fact-Finding Task Force to Inform and Guide Us on Whether to Expand Our Program to the Fast-Growing West Side Suburbs.

We had appointed a blue-ribbon group of famous academics to help us. We had world-renowned sociologists, geographers, psychologists, theologians, historians, philosophers, demographers, artists, engineers, dentists, and many other distinguished professors. Their charge was to examine the history, makeup, status, and trends of the West Side and advise us whether there was a role there for Our Organization in the twenty-first century.

Their timetable had been a full year and their budget seven times our original estimate.

Because they were about six months late and proportionately over budget, we were particularly eager to receive their final report, containing cogent findings and recommendations. Therefore, we were a bit surprised and disappointed to learn early in the presentation that after eighteen months, they hadn't yet been to the West Side and weren't even ready to look at the overall metropolitan area. It was also unsettling that most of the money had been spent on consultant fees (the expertise of the Task Force members was donated, but they could only be expected to formulate the questions that then had to be addressed by hired consultants, many of whom they were also), international travel ("to get the big picture and to learn from other cultures"), and out-of-town meetings ("Though we are all from this area, it is essential to such interdisciplinary examinations to create real distance in order to get used to each other's persons and disciplines").

But I get ahead of myself and their presentation.

Their primary messages were these:

1. They are turning up some tantalizing data (for example, on the relationship between neighbor islands in the South Pacific).

2. They need to add more researchers to the team (such as arctic geophysicists).
3. They need more time (they are still in something called the "environmental scan").
4. They need more money (lots of it).

To give us some flavor of their efforts to date, and perhaps to assuage our obvious disappointment, the Task Force Chairman, Dr. Percival Stonington, a noted professor of anthropology, pointed out why "spreading such a broad net has relevance. For example, to understand the West Side as an entity and its problems as a micromanifestation of the macro, one needs to study the universe of which they are a part."

Respectfully and warily, Rev. Horsinger asked if it wasn't also possible to approach it from the other side— "for example, by identifying the characteristics and problems of the West Side and comparing them to other sections of our area? And couldn't it also make sense to involve representatives of the community to be sure the assumptions and preliminary findings are accurate?"

Trying to be respectful that the Reverend might be an educated person, Prof. Stonington responded to the first part, about where to start: "It's not unusual for a layperson to think that could be so, but, of course, it would be absurd."

To spread the participation, he referred the second part of the question to his co-chair, Dr. Margaret McNaughton, a prizewinning musicologist who was not so diplomatic: "It is laughable and wildly unscientific to consult the objects of one's study. Any scientifically trained person would understand that it would contaminate the process and the findings to involve the involved. Also, to test our findings with community representatives would bring politics into the very arena where it least belongs."

In an effort to soften those answers, Prof. Stonington assured us that "prior to publication, reports will be made to community leaders so that they can get credit for early approval of our findings."

Unfortunately, the usually unflappable Reverend responded somewhat impatiently, "Forgive me, but as an educator and a man of the cloth, I worry that you and therefore we are falling into the trap of deciding what's best for people without being sure they agree."

Dr. McNaughton finished him off: "This is science and not some fuzzy, cozy, feely kind of counseling." (I was sorry to see Rev. Horsinger put down so, but he should have been more respectful.)

To retain the high ground, Prof. Stonington continued his lecture about why the fate of the West Side is connected to the rest of the world and why therefore any study of the community has to be approached globally. With the patience of a kindergarten teacher, he explained that the West Side is connected to the city, which in turn is connected to the metropolitan area, which in turn is connected to the state, the region, the nation, and on and on.

Mr. Wenski tried to give it a lighter touch by suggesting, "Sounds like the toe bone's connected to the foot bone, the foot bone's connected to the ankle bone . . ." but before he could carry the litany to the thigh bone, the professor interrupted, "I suppose one could look at it that way, but we don't." He then continued in more scholarly vernacular, "This series of interconnectedness carries all the way to the globe, the interplanetary system, outer space, and beyond."

Still smarting, Rev. Horsinger interjected, "Sounds to me like you'll need to decide between the creationists and the big bang theorists before you can understand our little West Side."

Dr. McNaughton responded defensively but definitely, "We will decide on the basis of facts and only the facts, and if there are some hypothetical questions that seem relevant but are not yet reduced to fact, we will conclude our paper with an indication of what additional research is needed, including, if necessary, the truth of creation and its influence on the stars, the sky, the mountains, the oceans, and all the way down to this frumpy little town and its scraggly West Side."

Even Mr. Scala, who has only an A.A. degree, didn't think that sounded very objective and said so out loud. The music doctor (or whatever she is) explained, "I'm not used to talking to such people, and I let my standards slip, so I should apologize." (Later, we couldn't decide if she had apologized for letting her standards slip by speaking to us or if she was genuinely sorry and sincere. In any case, we voted that we didn't like her professionally or personally but we wouldn't let it interfere with our ability to work with her. Rev. Horsinger, who should have voted with us and wanted to vote against us, abstained.)

All in all, what we hoped might be an exhilarating evening was turning out quite the reverse. It would probably have gotten even worse if our guests hadn't provided an escape when they said they needed an immediate resolution to the money matters, beginning with back payments "for all the work completed to date." Knowing that we still had to take up the reports of our Treasurer and our Development Committee, which were not likely to reveal encouraging balances, we insisted/begged for more time on the payments and tabled consideration of additional research until later ("The next century or the one after," suggested you know who).

With possible consideration of the payments already overdue and hoped for, Prof. Stonington bid a cordial good night and shook hands all around, but Dr. McNaughton said only, "It's been a memorable experience," and hurried away.

I'll bet that from now on, we'll always be able to overcome tough differences of opinion and even raise smiles from antagonists by singing softly, "The toe bone's connected to the foot bone, the foot bone's connected to the ankle bone, the ankle bone's connected to the thigh bone . . ." all the way up to the head bone. And by the time we get to "Hear ye the way of the Lord," we'll all be in a good mood.

Hear ye,
Mrs. Jeffrey (Effie) Black,
Secretary of the Board of Directors

11

Minutes of Our December Board Meeting

The meeting was opened at 8:30 P.M. because we kept waiting, hoping that Mr. Gonzalez would arrive with the Treasurer's report.

"The coward's not going to show up," shouted Mr. Shapiro.

"Maybe he's coming with Mr. Wenski," suggested Mrs. Pepper.

"We can't wait that long!" exclaimed Mrs. Greenlaw.

Mr. Russell could tell he had a tougher than usual meeting on his hands and moved aggressively to take charge. "I assure you all, we are going to have a Treasurer's report, even if Mr. Gonzalez doesn't show up. We'll give him another ten minutes and then ask Jack to review the financial statements for him. I also assure you that we are going to have the executive session to review the Executive Secretary's performance." Jack interrupted imploringly, "Do you think it's fair to ask me to do the Treasurer's report and still have my evaluation?"

"Sounds like a perfect combination," responded Mr. Colberg eagerly.

With that, Mr. Russell returned to the proper order of business and called for a reading of the minutes of our last meeting. Perhaps it was because the minutes had been a source of so much upset recently or perhaps it was a reflection of important business still to come, but in any case there was no discussion of the minutes. Mr. Russell was so taken with surprise that he remained occupied with his pocket calculator for a good ninety seconds before it suddenly hit him that there was absolute silence in response to the minutes. He explained that he had settled in to do his monthly expense report and apologized that he hadn't realized that something was wrong.

Mr. Russell looked around and, not spotting the Treasurer, asked Jack Neal if he would summarize our financial position. White as a sheet, Jack pleaded, "Mr. Gonzalez still has four minutes."

"In that case, let's undertake the executive session," suggested Mr. Russell.

"Do you have to call it an undertaking?" implored Jack, whose pale white had become a spotted blue green with a few patches of bruised pink.

"I assure you, we'll give you your just due," comforted Mrs. Mitchell. "Perfectly said," topped Mr. Shapiro.

As Jack and his Office Manager, Administrative Assistant, Assistant Secretary, and Assistant Treasurer, Paula Masonowitz, left the room, the Board members rearranged their chairs into a tight circle, and with each scrape of a chair, Jack's stomach got tighter, too. When he reached the door, Paula helped him through.

Before we actually began, Mr. Russell had me peek out each door to be sure Jack wasn't listening in.

The discussion started positively enough. For the first several minutes there was silence. In the next ten minutes there were some nice things said. For example, both Mr. Yarborough and Mrs. Archer commented on how hard Jack works. Mr. Zukert responded, "I know he works hard, but I'm not sure what he does all that time."

If it's not confusing metaphors, from that point the roller coaster started down and the fur began to fly. Twice I had to go out and ask the staff to move farther away to put them out of earshot of the shrill voices.

This being an executive session, the minutes don't have to be as complete as I'm generally noted for, but for future reference I will provide some flavor of the discussion, a summary of the points we seemed to agree on, and our conclusion.

1. *Flavor.* Some people like him and some don't.

In the past, Jack has expressed the view that Mr. Colberg and Mr. Shapiro are out to get him. It's true.

It's not that a lot of people actively dislike Jack or disapprove of what he does. There's just a vague sense of his worthlessness.

On balance, he has his defenders, but when pressed for specifics, they tend to point out things like "nice teeth" or "not many people in these jobs went to prep school" or "you don't remember the last one!"

2. *Generally agreed observations.* We want an Executive to take charge but not usurp the Board's responsibilities and prerogatives.

Our Executive should be a more forceful spokesman for the organization but not get out front.

An Executive should come to committee and Board meetings with crisp recommendations for all the action items but should not talk too much.

A good Executive should spend more time in the office "and less on all that outside junk."

"Jack should get out and do more and not spend all his time behind that big desk."

A good Executive should be more confident and aggressive but definitely not assertive.

We need a real leader who can tell us what to do and make us do it but know his subordinate place in the organization.

He should look more like an Executive ("If only we could get him to wear suits with vests"), but he should come across more as a charity worker ("Maybe I can find him an old cross to wear," Rev. Horsinger volunteered).

We need someone who has skills in fundraising, management, organizing, budgeting, PR, program direction, public speaking, planning, evaluation, proposal writing, office management, and community networking and who has such personal attributes as leadership abilities, pleasant manner, good looks, unflappability, and the ability to get along with everybody ("Maybe I could find an even larger cross that he can carry!" concluded the Reverend).

To be fair, we agreed that it is unreasonable to want our Executive to have all these skills and qualities, but there was considerable disagreement about what qualities Jack has. ("He doesn't have a damn one!" accused Mr. Shapiro. "That's not fair," protested

Mrs. Workenthrader. "Name two," challenged Mr. Colberg. Mrs. Workenthrader stumbled slightly but finally blurted out, "Well, at least he comes to all the meetings." But no sooner was it out than she realized that some might spot a negative in it. She started to try again, but the flow was against her.)

3. *Our conclusions.* After about an hour of scalding candor, during which I twice went out to assure Jack that we were just into some miscellaneous matters off the track, our Chairperson said it was time to try to pull it all together. This was not altogether well received. Some people were clearly enjoying the free-spiritedness of the trial, and others were uncomfortable with what it might lead to. Finally, Mr. Fales stepped in with "There's no sense in cutting him up anymore. It's pretty obvious we have to let him go."

More than half the Board members were on their feet protesting that Fales had totally misread the discussion. Mrs. Mitchell was heard above the others crying, "Oh my God, that's not what we've been saying at all. We've just been adding up all his faults and shortcomings and just because there are so many of them doesn't mean we would be disloyal to him."

Mr. Colberg tried to be analytical. "If we had been keeping a tally with his strengths on one side and weaknesses on the other, we'd have thirty-two pages of black marks and only nice teeth going for him."

"Don't forget 'working hard,'" added Mrs. Pepper.

"Maybe the problem is we don't pay him enough," said Ms. Trister. "You know, it's a proven fact that people respond positively to confidence and fairness."

"I can't believe this," said Mr. Colberg apoplectically, but his analytical approach was giving way to the mysticism of collective judgment, where kind hearts and cold feet outweigh logic every time.

While four people were on their feet protesting that the discussion required bold action, the majority formulated a motion that would give Jack a 10 percent raise while putting him on probation until at least a few of his gross inadequacies showed evidence of turnaround.

The warring between a clear majority and an intransigent minority might have gone on indefinitely, but it was at that moment that Mr. Gonzalez showed up, and Mr. Russell seized the diversion to declare a sense of the meeting and called for a recess "while we regroup for Gonzalez." It was probably true that our Treasurer had not turned up earlier out of fear of the consequences, for he responded to our Chairperson's "regrouping" with stark terror in every line of his face.

Sometimes a short recess is called a comfort break. This was not one of them. Perhaps the most uncomfortable was Jack Neal, who was told only that the executive session had ended so we could take up the Treasurer's report. Compared to him, Mr. Gonzalez was a model of composure.

It was clear at the start that bad news was coming when Mr. Gonzalez began with the reminder that "it's not fair to shoot the messenger." We also knew we were in trouble when Mr. Gonzalez kept referring to himself as our Banker and not as our Treasurer. The last time that happened, every Board member had to pony up his or her share of the overdraft.

I'll say this for our Treasurer: He didn't mince words. He put it to us this way:

Ladies and gentlemen, you have been clobbered by a quadruple whammy.

One. The Cutting-Edge and Fail-Safe Foundation has turned you down because the organization is not well enough established with a proven track record.

Two. The United Way has turned you down because this is not an emerging organization.

Three. No bequest or memorial gift has come in because nobody has died yet who believes the organization is beyond "emerged" but still "unproven."

Four. Not one person has thought that what we do is worth purchasing.

In conclusion, Our Organization is figuratively and literally worthless.

Each point was enunciated with escalating gravity, pitch, tremor, and timber, ending in one of our Treasurer's classic solos. "You are broke, zeroed out, creditless, down the tube, penniless . . ." But by the time his performance reached full throttle, it had become triple harmony, with our Chairperson trying to shut him up and the Board adding its own response so that it began to sound like a funeral dirge.

You are indebted.

OK, OK, we hear you.

Oh, my God.

You are destitute.

OK, OK, that's enough.

What will happen to us?

You are ruined.

Please, you've made your point.

We're all liable.

You're on the street.

We've got your message loud and clear.

Can they attach our homes?

You're bottoms up.

Stop it, Harry!

That's what comes of being volunteers.

But neither Mr. Russell nor the full Board was a match for the person posing as a Treasurer in Banker's clothing. "You're through, finished, awash in red ink, bad risks, fiscally embarrassed, financial bummers; the wolf's at the door . . ." he trilled until he dropped exhausted into his seat and the whole congregation wept with the physical exertion and meaning of it all.

Mr. Zukert was the first to recover and pleaded, "Can it really be that bad?" But when Mr. Gonzalez started to get to his feet, Mr. Russell cut him off with words that shall not be included in my minutes.

Mrs. Lortz asked our Treasurer if he "had a ballpark figure as to what it would cost each Board member to make things right."

"In the neighborhood of ten to fifteen thou."

And this time the responses from the chorus outlasted any litany that even Mr. Gonzalez could string together. It was at this point that Mr. Wenski arrived and profusely begged forgiveness: "I was collecting door to door for the Cancer Society and just kept getting into long conversations."

"How much did you get?" asked Mrs. O'Reilly.

"Forty-one dollars and seventy-five cents," beamed the proud Mr. Wenski.

"Put it on the table along with everything else you've got," demanded Mr. Horton.

"What is this, a holdup?" asked the incredulous Mr. Wenski.

"Far worse, much worse, a thousand times worse," started Mr. Gonzalez, but Mr. Russell broke in and explained the situation to our late arrival, whose blanched, drained panic now blended with everyone else's.

We realized that our October retreat had not begun to test our creative thinking. With our backs to the wall, we would somehow raise the money.

One scheme seemed to offer a sure out. Mrs. Lortz explained that the way a lot of the rich agencies get their money is to testify before the county board and sometimes even the state legislature on behalf of the government agency that is their counterpart, like the health agency and health department. By being the government agency's citizens' lobby, appropriations are protected and usually increased, and then the voluntary group applies for just a tiny fraction for its own work, which is, of course, to be the citizens' lobby.

"Oh, I know all about that," said Mr. Zukert. "Some organizations have even carried it to the extreme of an informal agreement that they get one percent of the appropriations."

"I hear the Headache Society is up to two and seven-eighths percent," joined Mrs. Workenthrader.

"What happens if the citizens' lobby wants to cut appropriations or doesn't think its government counterpart is doing a good job?" cautioned Rev. Horsinger.

"And cut off its lifeline?" scoffed Mr. Wenski, now totally caught up in the practicalities.

"Could this be called lobbying?" tested Mr. Colberg.

"A few get into trouble, but most cover it under public education," assured Mrs. Archer.

"And what if someone uncovered the fact that we were involved with a quid pro quo?" persisted Rev. Horsinger.

"Nobody said anything about the Mafia," reacted Mrs. O'Reilly.

Undeterred, the Reverend bore in. "But wouldn't it look terrible if we were found to sell our testimony for a fixed portion of the agency's appropriation?"

"Oh, it's nothing that obvious," assured Mrs. Archer. "It's just understood that your applications get fair treatment that happens to average out around one percent."

"I still don't like it," our moralist intoned. "There's nobody more hard pressed than I even to dream of coming up with fifteen thousand dollars, but it's one thing to go to jail as a pauper and another to get sent there for a shady scheme."

Mrs. Archer responded with shrieks of injured honor, but the prospect of double jeopardy had sobered the discussion.

Though at first it didn't seem like an adequate response to the crisis, we found ourselves back on the old subject of a Special Event.

The idea of a dance or ball was resurrected but got little more enthusiasm than it had in the past. "Besides," I said, "my husband would be a little suspicious if so soon after the retreat, I told him we had decided to have a dance. He is still probing what went on out at Camp Bluebird."

"Why is it that so many other organizations make so much money on their society balls?" wondered Mrs. Greenlaw.

Jack Neal responded thoughtfully, "It helps to start with a Board that glitters with names, money, and connections," and was in trouble all over again.

"Didn't we once try a walkathon?" asked Mr. Horton. "Yes, I'm afraid we did," replied Mr. Russell, "and further, I'm afraid we set it on the same day and track as the Leukemia Society's bikathon, and so many of our people got run down and cut up that it cost us more than we made."

"We seem to be good at that," added Mr. Gonzalez.

Undiscouraged, Ms. Trister said that maybe we should try one of the current gimmicks that involves a "nonevent," "where you assure people they don't have to go to a stuffy ball or some other special event, and out of appreciation and charitable impulse, they contribute the same amount of money and often much more."

Mr. Colberg said, "It sure would fit our pattern of activities where nobody shows up anyway."

Mrs. Mitchell splashed the final cold water by saying that by the time she had come to the organization, we had such a reputation for nonevents that we'd best not call unfortunate attention to ourselves.

Again, out of the innocence of newness and attractive enthusiasm, Ms. Trister asked if we had ever tried a chili cook-off, but the second she saw Mr. Peter Paul Henderson's face go pale and jaw go slack, she regretted it.

Fortunately, the moment passed, and with it any further bright ideas, so Mr. Shapiro said that maybe we would just have to kick in the money, which stimulated a lot of violent body language, if not brainstorms.

As inevitably happens in such discussions, someone recalled our last carnival and made the mistake of mentioning it. Though it was six years ago, events are still too recent and raw to be remembered with anything like

nostalgia or humor. Some circumstances had taken us a
long time to overcome, like the mayor and his wife's getting stuck on top of the Ferris wheel, the school super-
intendent being hit in the fanny by a dart that missed a
balloon by 180 degrees, the wind tunnel blowing the
hairpiece off the President of the Chamber of Commerce, and the Chief of Police's claiming to have gotten
pyorrhea from our kissing booth.

With surprising insensitivity, Mr. Shapiro suggested
bingo, but Mrs. O'Reilly scotched that by assuring the
group that "Father Scallon would be absolutely furious
with our competition, and I have enough trouble getting through his confessions without a two-hour novena
as it is."

Our always creative head of the Public Relations
Committee, Pat Greenlaw, came up with the novel idea of
a scavenger hunt, but she inadvertently stepped on her own
idea when she suggested that we could include a search to
find the first person ever served by Our Organization.

Mrs. Lortz said, "That might get rather expensive
because we'd probably have to give everybody a shovel."

"That's not fair!" screamed Mr. Peter Paul Henderson.

"Besides," seconded Jack Neal, "our services have
gotten much better."

It was another example of a good idea being lost to a
bad "for instance."

We covered the ground of bake sales, art auctions, and just about every conceivable product or service we might peddle. Someone else was already doing it, or we had tried it and failed, or the investment made it too risky for even this desperate group.

We covered grapefruit, flowers, dishes, casseroles, cookies, candy, Bibles, magazines, airplane rides, and every known fruit, vegetable, sweet, or adventure, but someone was already there.

Next we tried the tack of special days, but someone has beaten us to Valentine's Day, Thanksgiving, Easter, Christmas, and, according to the clearinghouse calendar, 850 other days of the year. The discussion was somewhat useful, though, because we thought of some things we might do for our bequest program on Memorial Day ("While you're remembering, remember us"). Someone had the novel idea of using people's birthdays ("Make our day—pass up your day"), but even though we agreed there was the bud of an idea there, we couldn't quite make it flower.

We were probably only an inch away from having to face putting up the money ourselves when Mr. Yarborough saved the day. He reminded us that in our discussions about networking and about applying to the United Way and to the Cutting-Edge and Fail-Safe Foundation we kept learning that our program falls between the slats of what other people are doing. He reminded us that we had come to realize that what we are trying to do has implications for art museums, high blood pressure, youth services, preservation, the elderly, unemployment, international understanding, and protection of the ozone layer, to name a few. "Wouldn't it make sense, then," he spun out with fascinating logic, "if we give up trying to raise money ourselves but simply ask all the organizations that already raise money for these causes to give us a piece of what they raise? With the breadth of our interest, we wouldn't have to ask for much. I've not really thought it out, but for organizations where there is a good deal of overlap, we could ask for maybe a third, and where it's only tangential, maybe as little as two or three percent."

"What if they won't give it to us?" asked Mr. Gonzalez pessimistically.

"I think they'll see the logic of it," interjected Mrs. Pepper.

"It's absolutely logical, and if they don't agree cooperatively," warned Mr. Scala, "we could politely suggest that we might have to conduct our own fundraising campaign for the same cause in the same week, and that should bring them around."

"This puts a whole new light on the concept of 'our fair share,'" said Mr. Knight optimistically. "We could even call the campaign 'Our Share of Your Share.'"

"I can remember the meetings when we sat around worrying about how much of what we were trying to do overlapped with some of the larger groups already in the community," put in Mrs. O'Reilly. "But with this concept, the greater the overlap, the more we can charge!" Mrs. Archer chimed in, "Our campaign theme could be 'Pay Your Overlap.'"

"And," enthused Pat Greenlaw, "it would look great in publicity to say that we worked in cooperation with the Red Cross, the Crippled Children's Society, the Nature Conservancy, the YMCA, the Council on Alcoholism, the Jewish Federation, the Mental Health Association, Meals on Wheels, the Asia Society, the Planetary Society, Presbyterian Hospital, and the United Negro College Fund. This is really big. This is absolutely fantastic."

Doubter Colberg, always the old stick-in-the-mud, still questioned whether these organizations would be amenable or could be persuaded to give up some of their hard-won contributions, but Mr. Knight said, "We might just have to play hardball." He said we'd have to go after the easiest ones first, and with successes behind us, we could then mow down the tougher ones. He even predicted that by the time we got our fair share of even half the groups with whom we overlap, we'd be bigger than the United Way and maybe even bigger than the Cutting-Edge and Fail-Safe Foundation. With renewed confidence, Mr. Wenski shouted, "Yeah, who needs them, anyway!"

Rev. Horsinger cautioned that our methods sounded as though they might border on blackmail or extortion, and he shuddered when we progressed to such expressions as "mowing them down."

Mr. Knight hastened to say that although some observers might describe our intentions as skimming and we had to be prepared to go to the mat with some folks, it was all in the name of charity. He also reminded the Reverend and the group as a whole that as a Board, we have a legal and moral responsibility to serve Our Organization.

The enthusiasm reached such a pitch that the group decided that perhaps we should try to knock off one of the big ones first, both to put ourselves on the map and, not incidentally, to solve the immediate shortfall. Mr. Fales was bold enough to suggest the Girl Scouts, and there was a collective gasp. That really tested our resolve and caused not a little review of our prospects. It was one thing to talk about the Symphony or even Saint Luke's Orphanage, but the ultimate in daring was to think of putting the arm on the Girl Scouts.

We were given a bit more courage with examples of how we could subtly suggest cutting into their sales or switching our backing to Camp Fire, and gradually our feet tingled with the itch to take them on.

As with all such crusades, we gained confidence from a marching song that Ms. Trister quickly composed.

Within moments, all of us had mastered the first stanza, and while she scribbled out the next ones, we circled the table, chanting:

> Scare a Scout!
> Skim the Scouts!
> Sis boom bah!
> Our Organization,
> Rah! Rah! Rah!

Mr. Peter Paul Henderson was not able to march with us, but he was clearly with us in spirit. With his eyes on the horizon and a drumbeat in his heart, he dared to whisper: "Maybe, just maybe, we could do the Knights of Columbus next."

On that note of optimism, the meeting was adjourned at 11:16 P.M.

> *Respectfully submitted,*
> *Mrs. Jeffrey (Effie) Black,*
> *Secretary of the Board of Directors*